This Notebook
Belongs to:

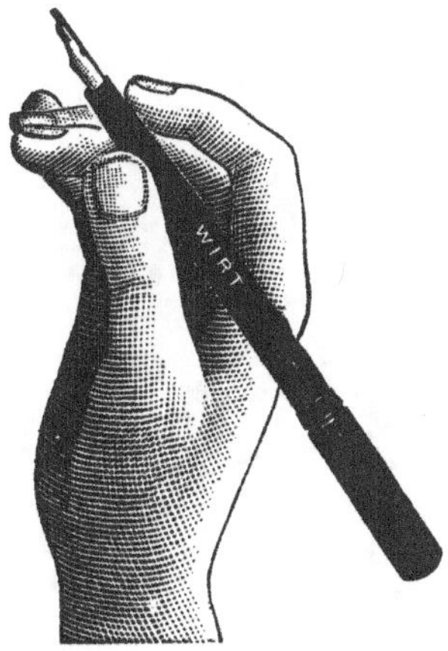

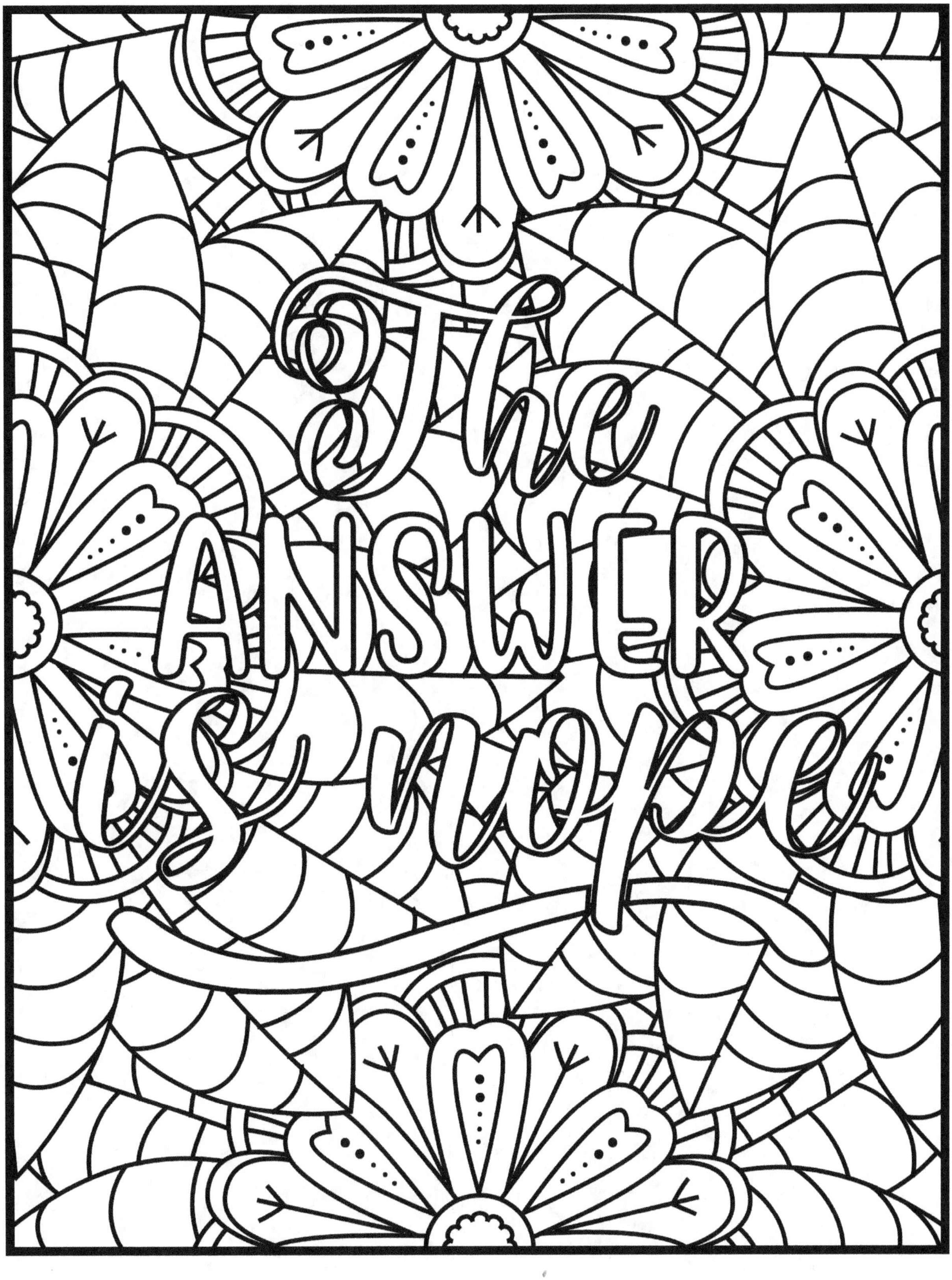
The
ANSWER
is nope

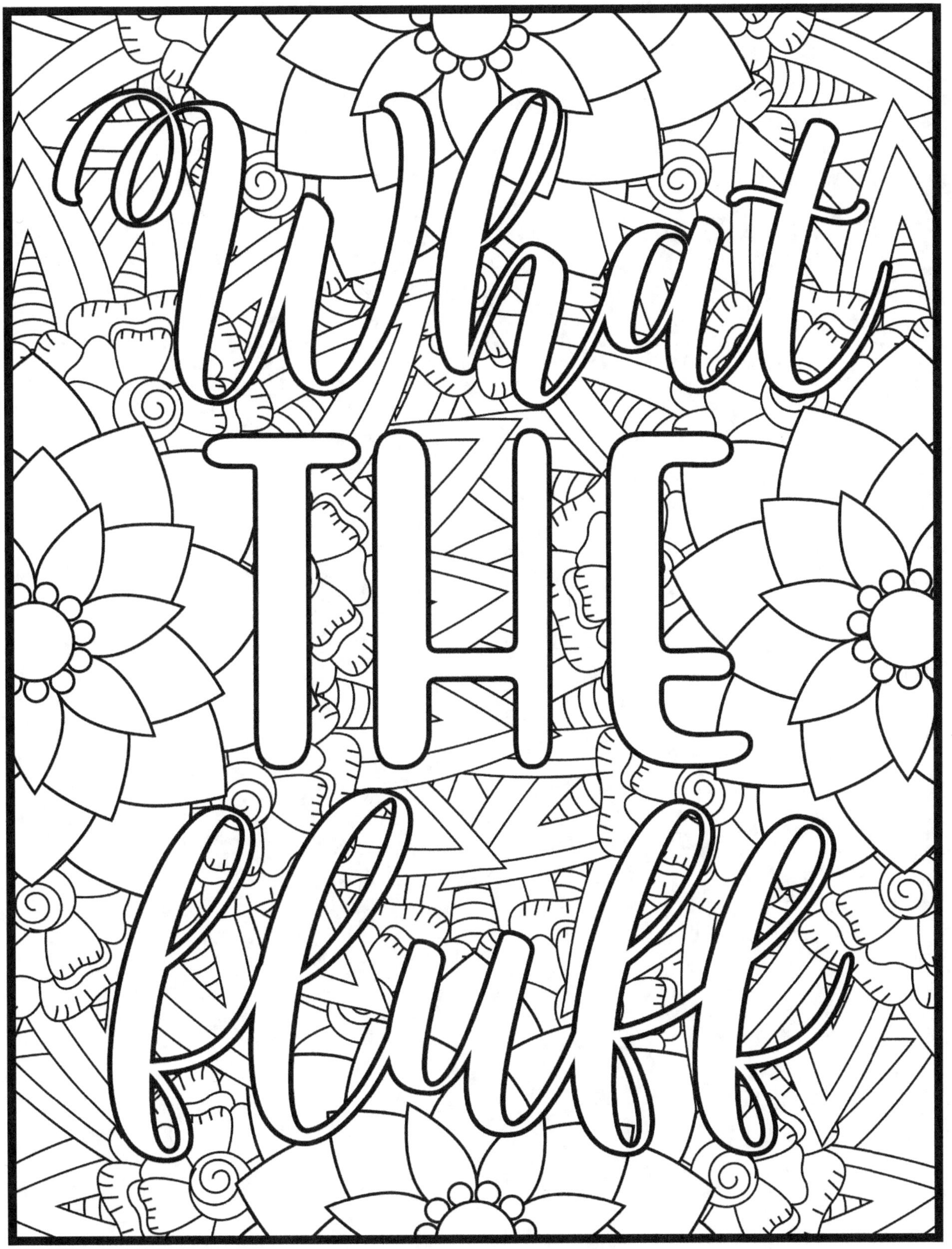
What
THE
fluff

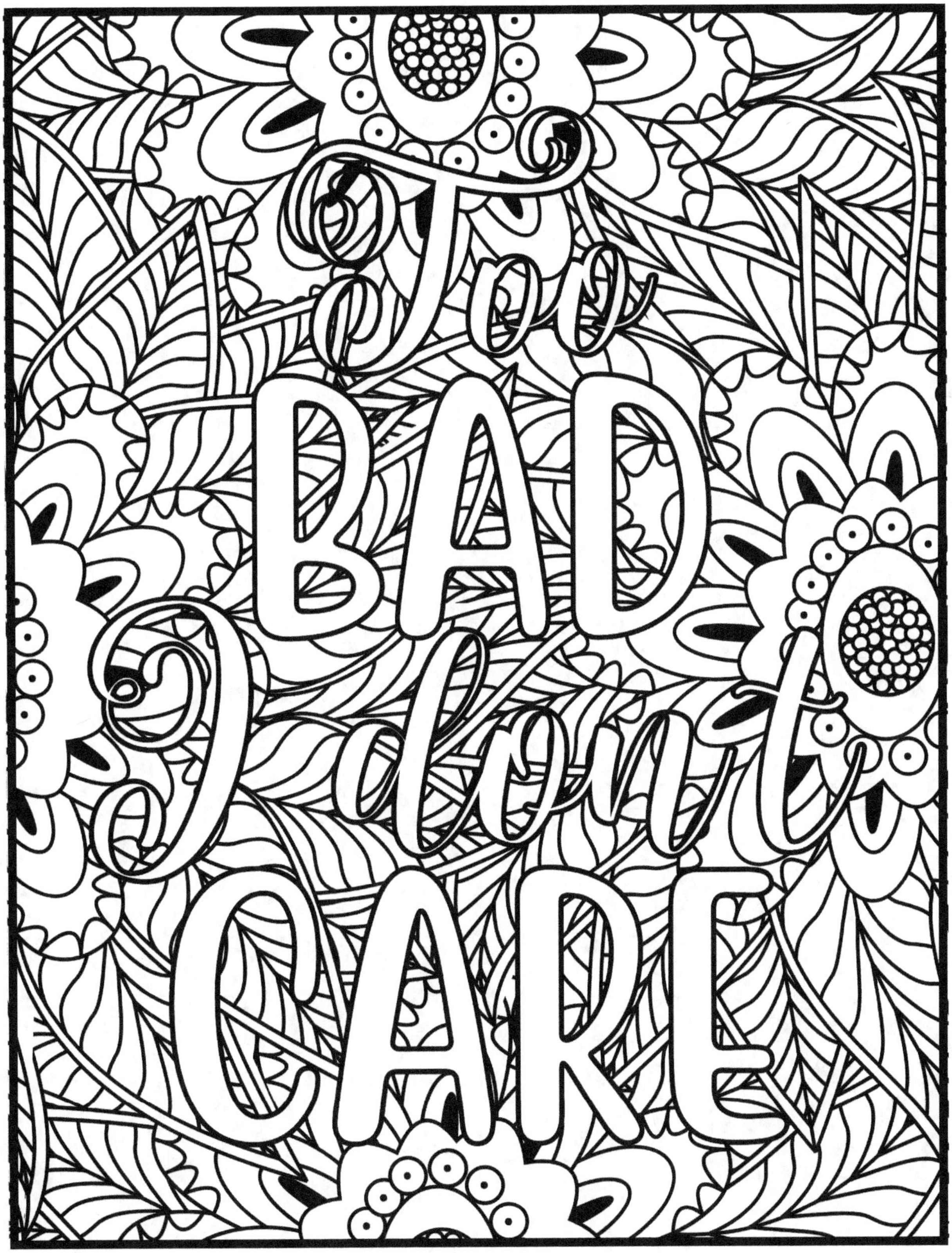
Too
BAD
I don't
CARE

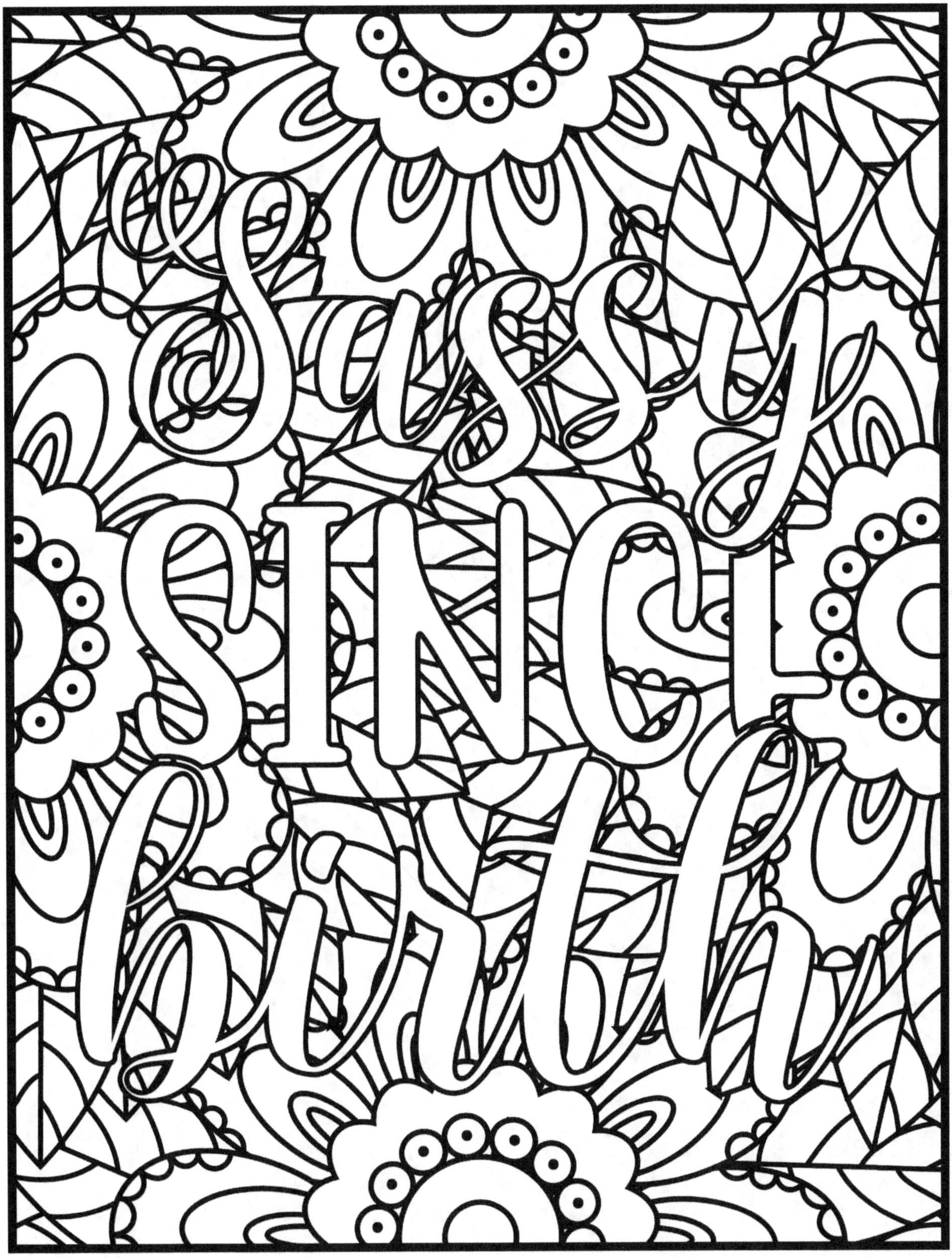
Sassy
SINCE
birth

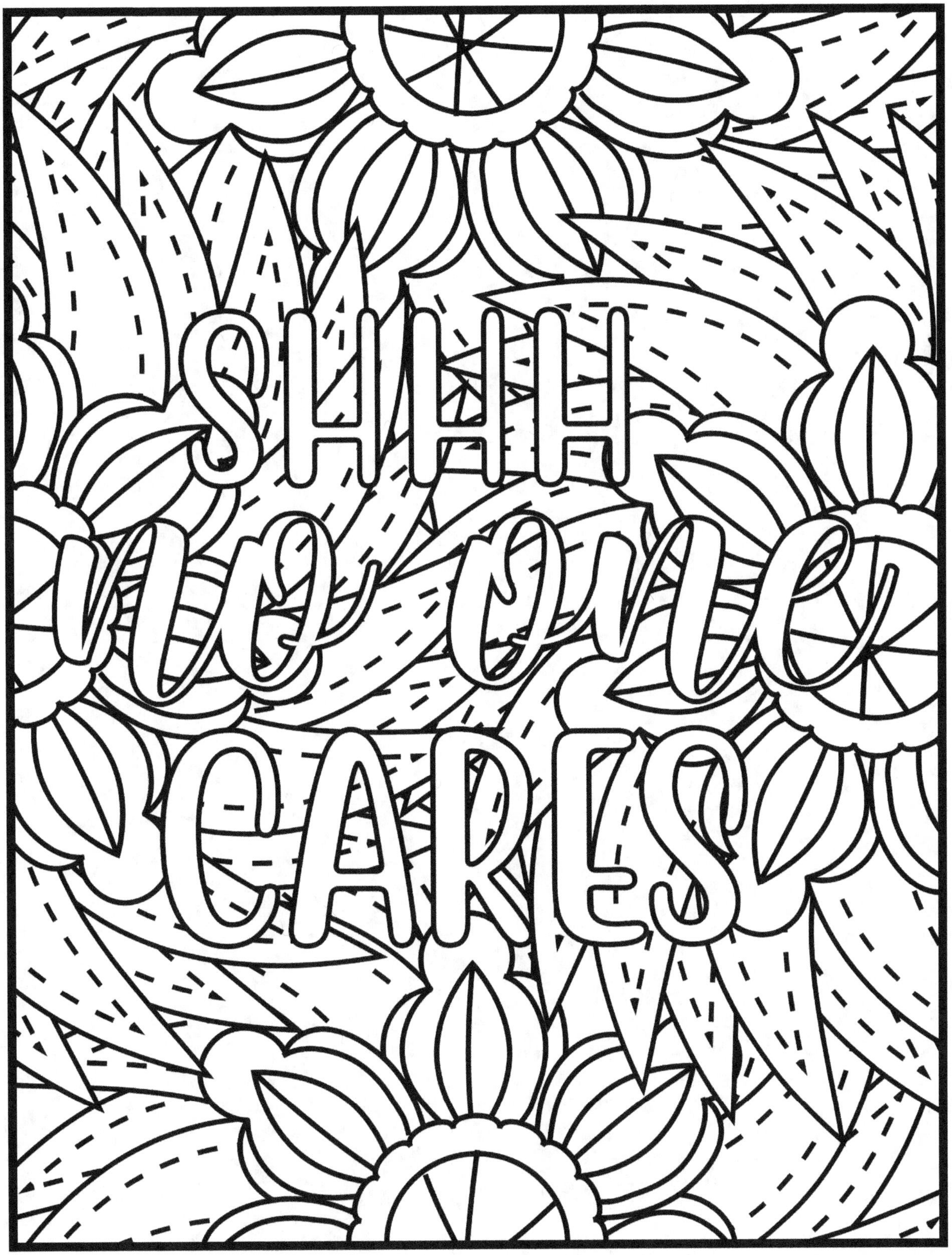
SHHH
no one
CARES

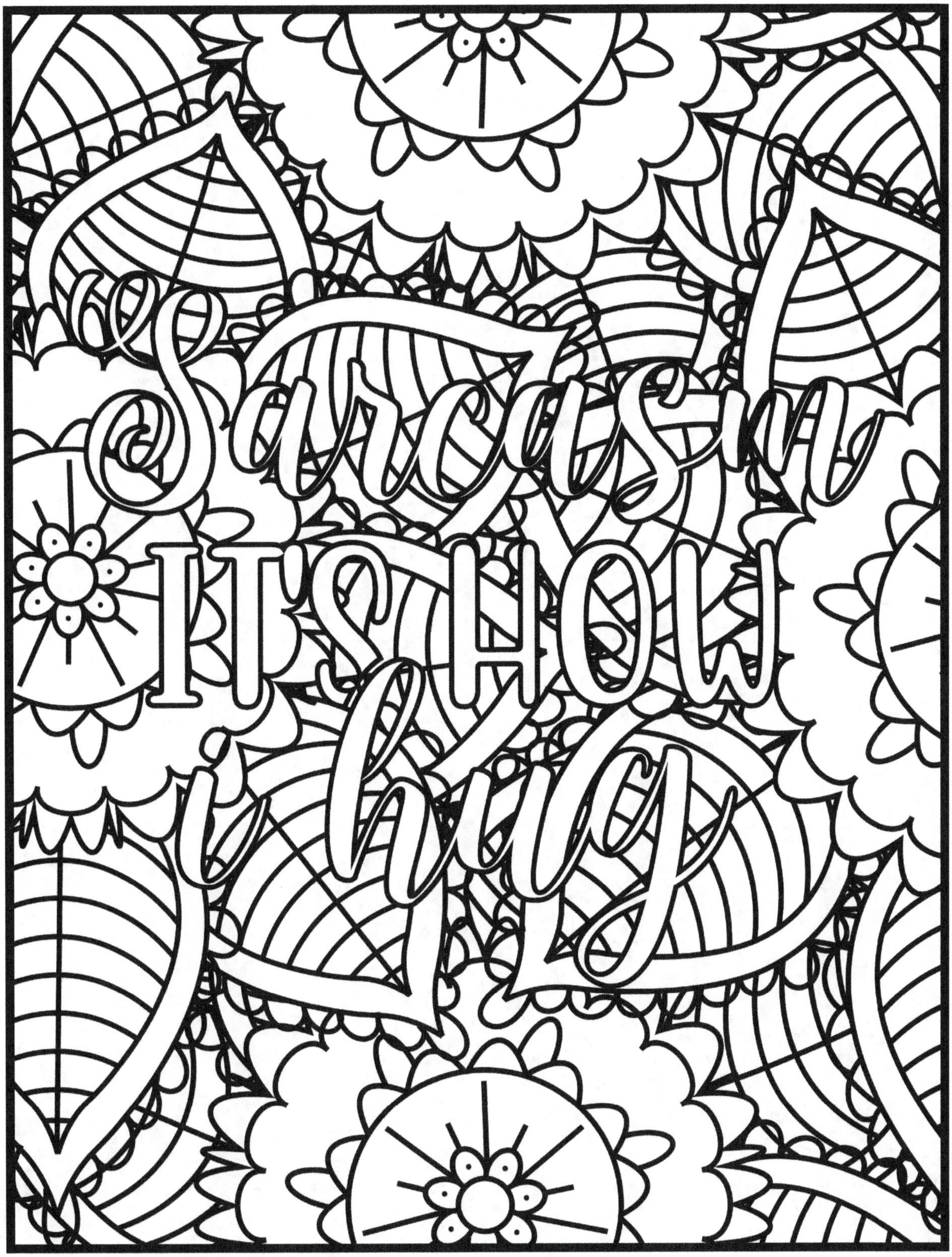
Sarcasm
IT'S HOW
i hug

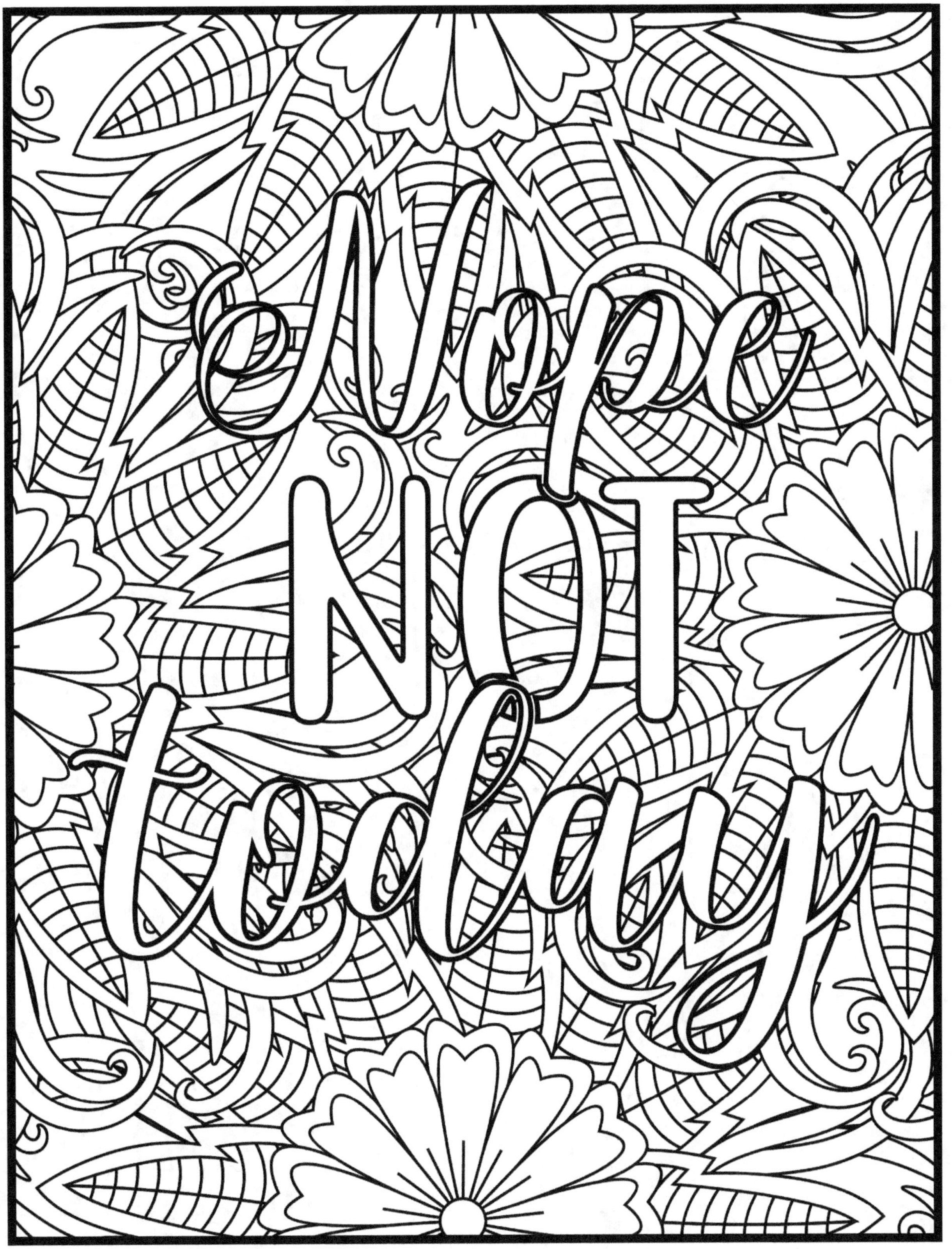
Nope
NOT
today

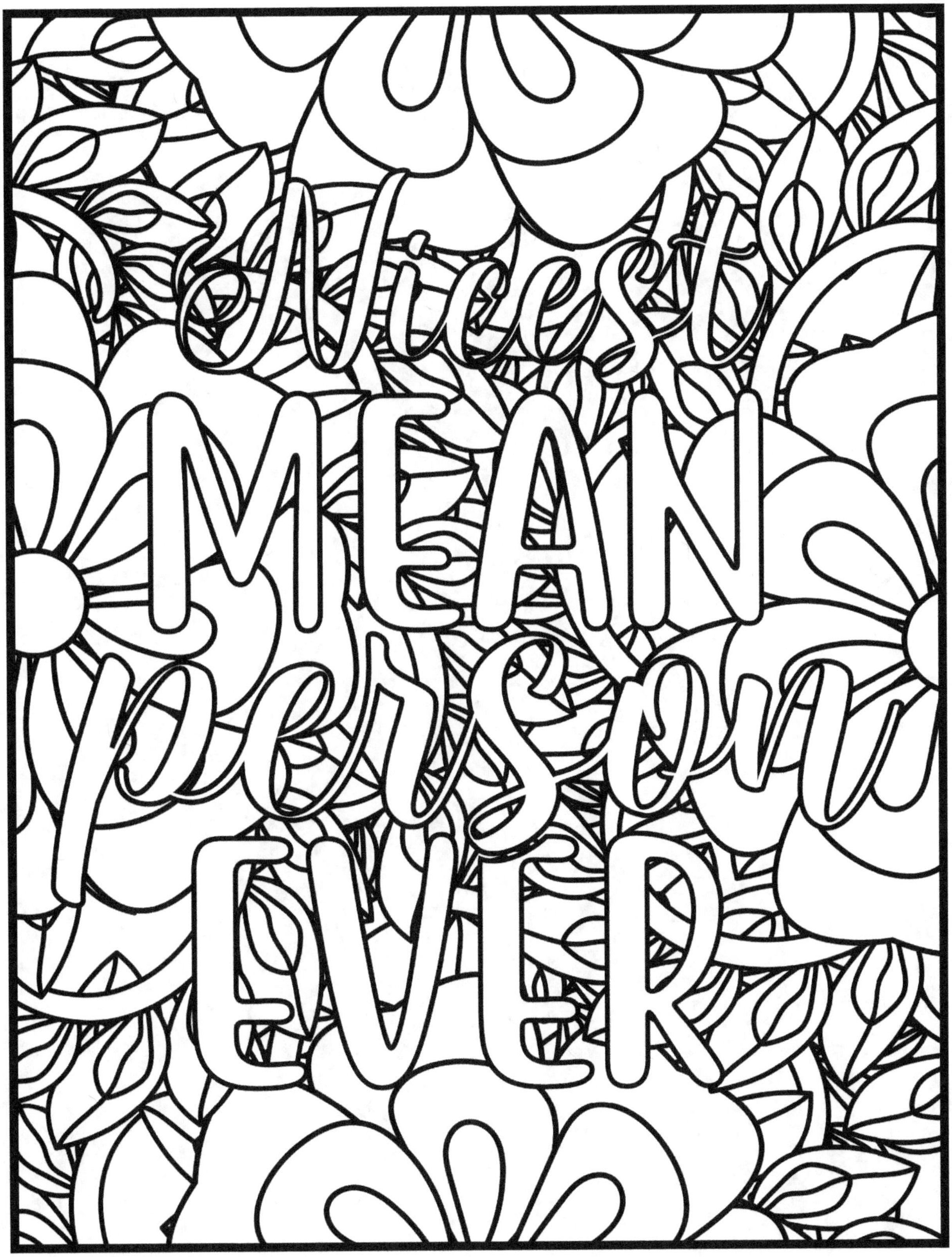
Nicest
MEAN
person
EVER

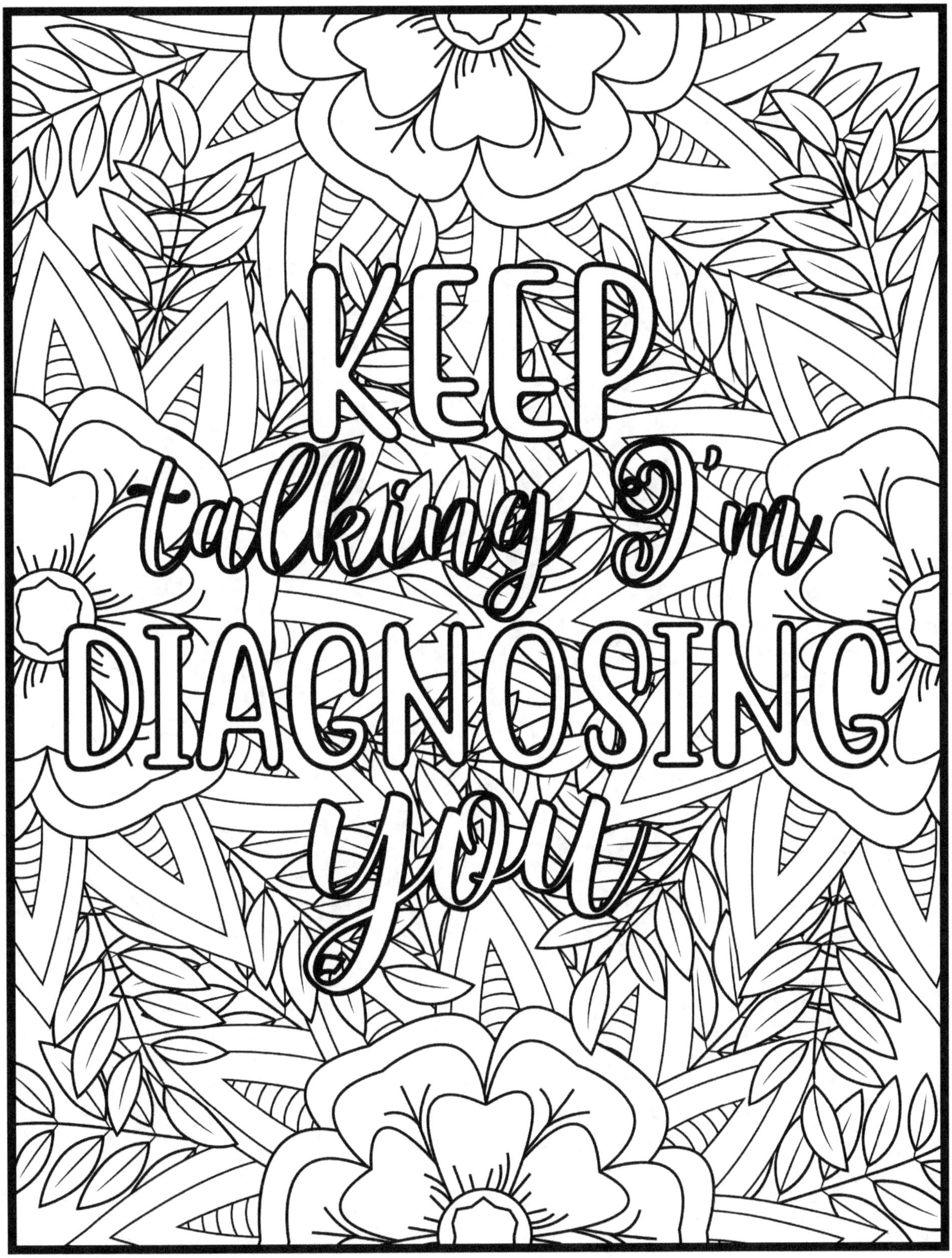
KEEP
talking I'm
DIAGNOSING
you

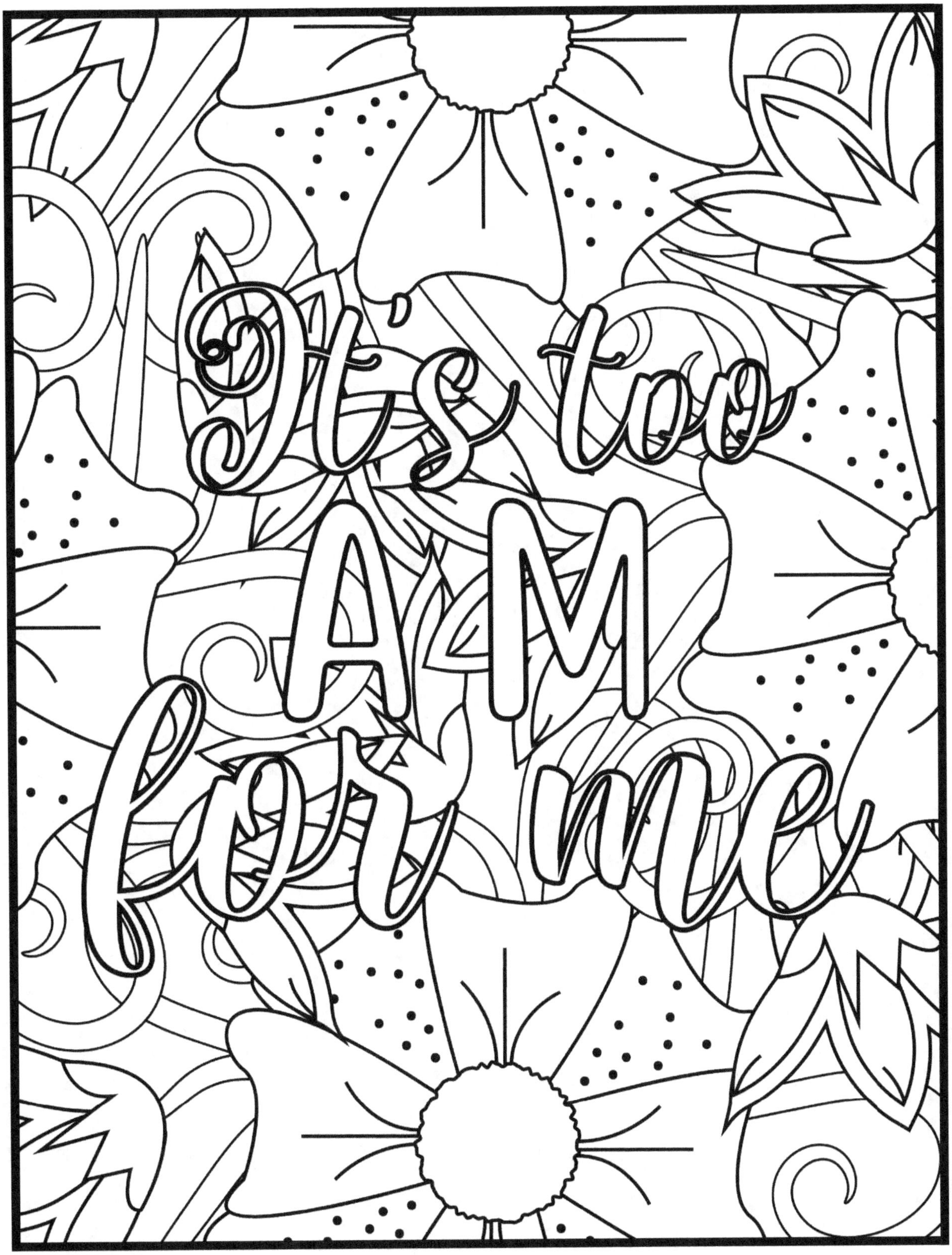
It's too
AM
for me

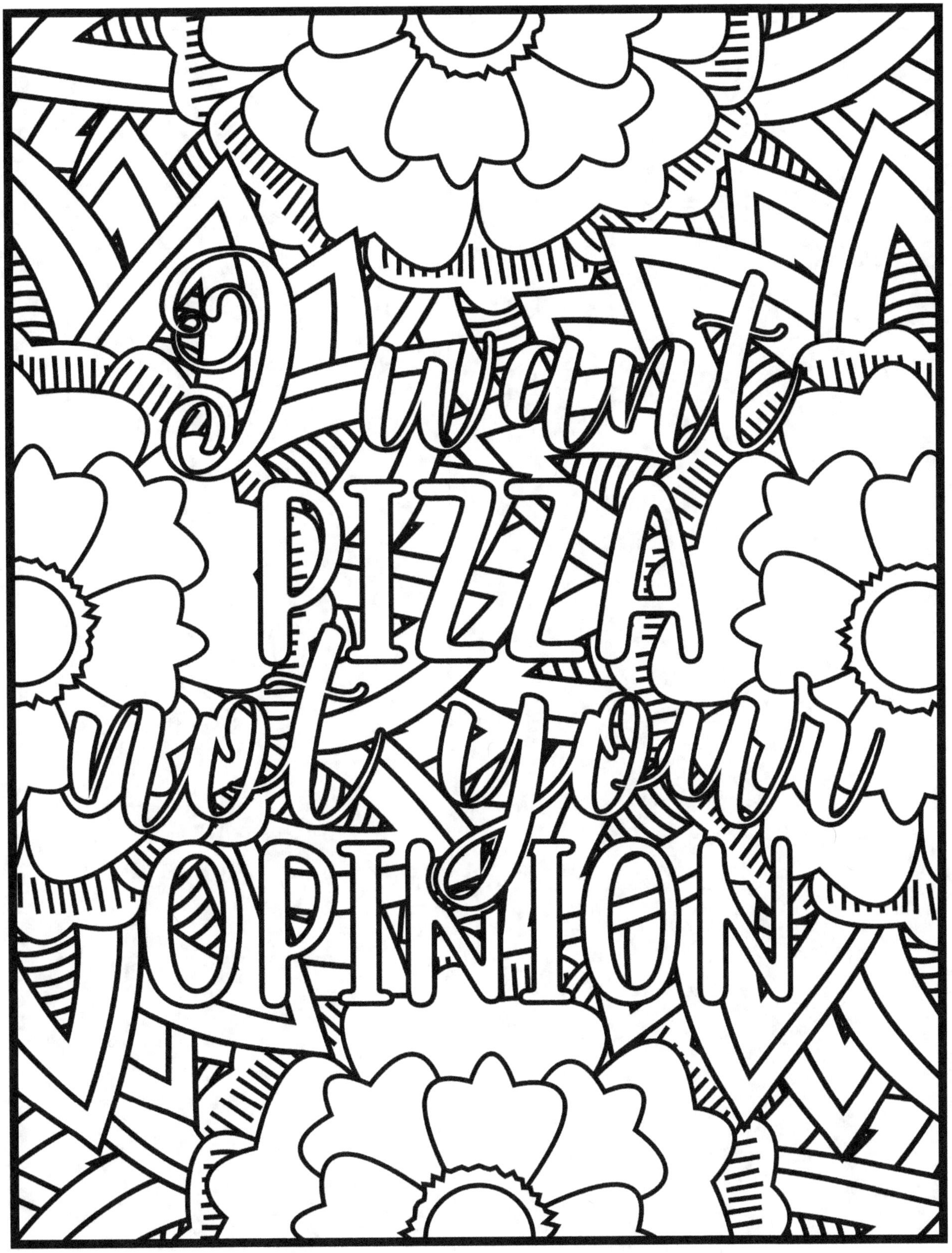
I want
PIZZA
not your
OPINION

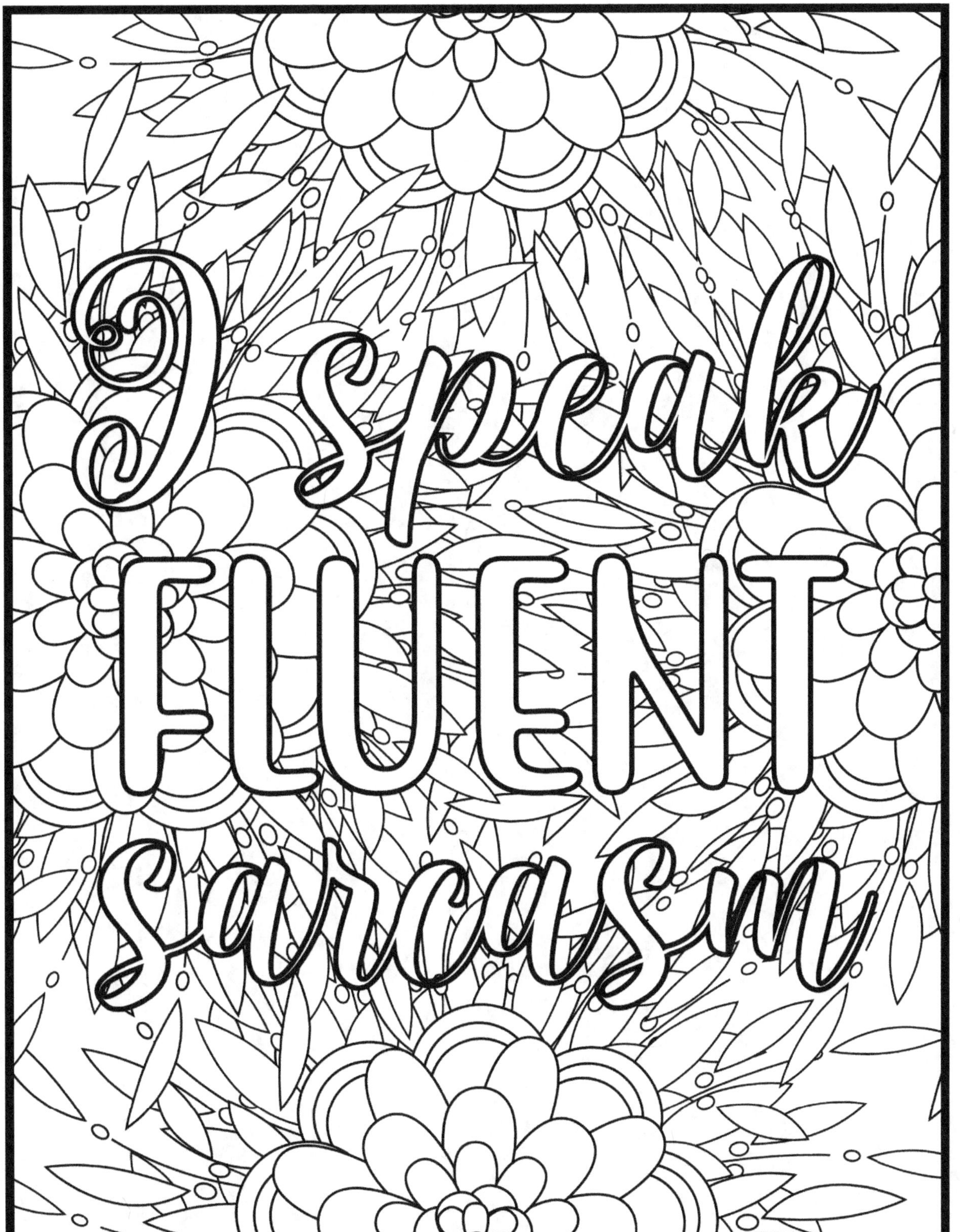
I speak
FLUENT
sarcasm

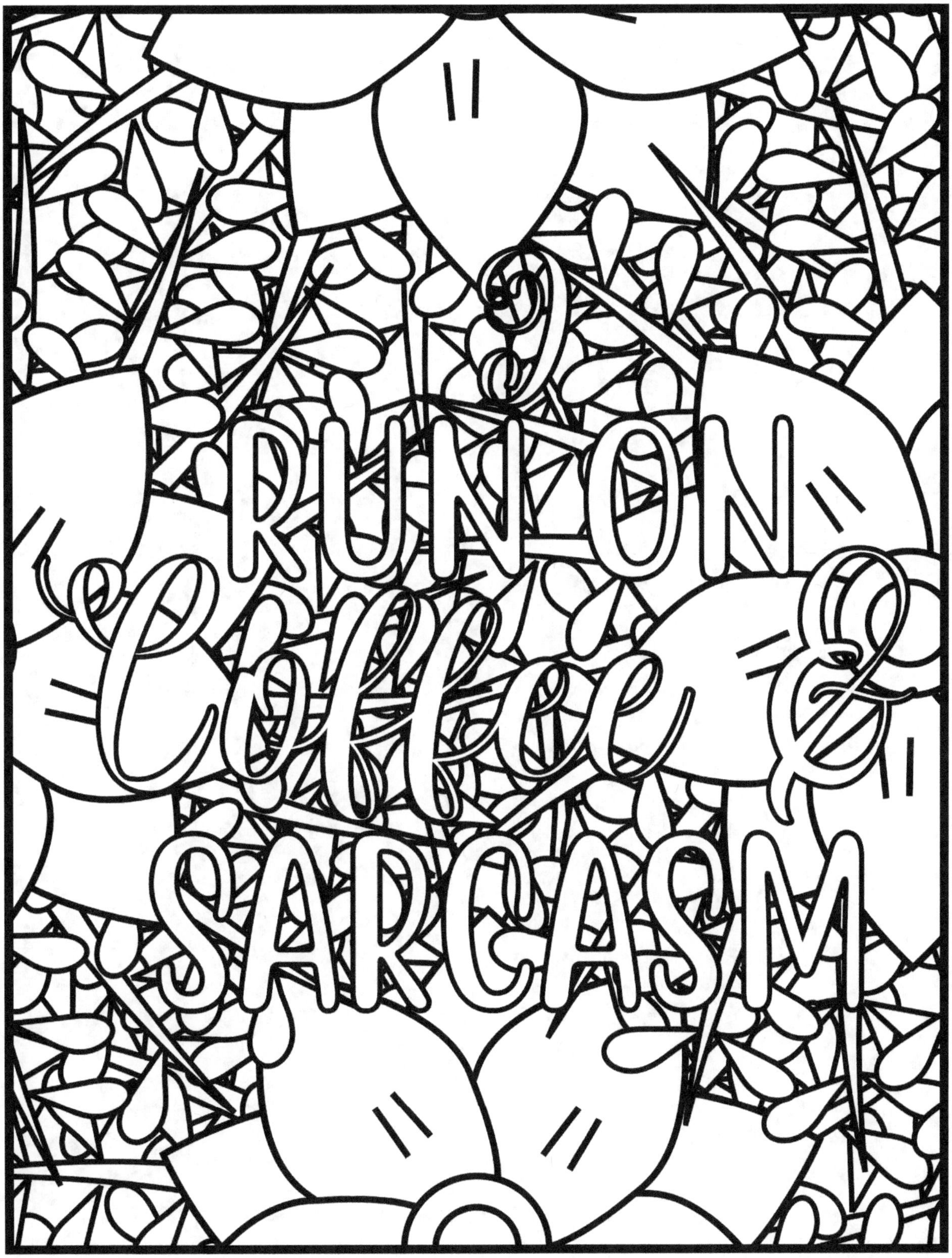
I
RUN ON
Coffee &
SARCASM

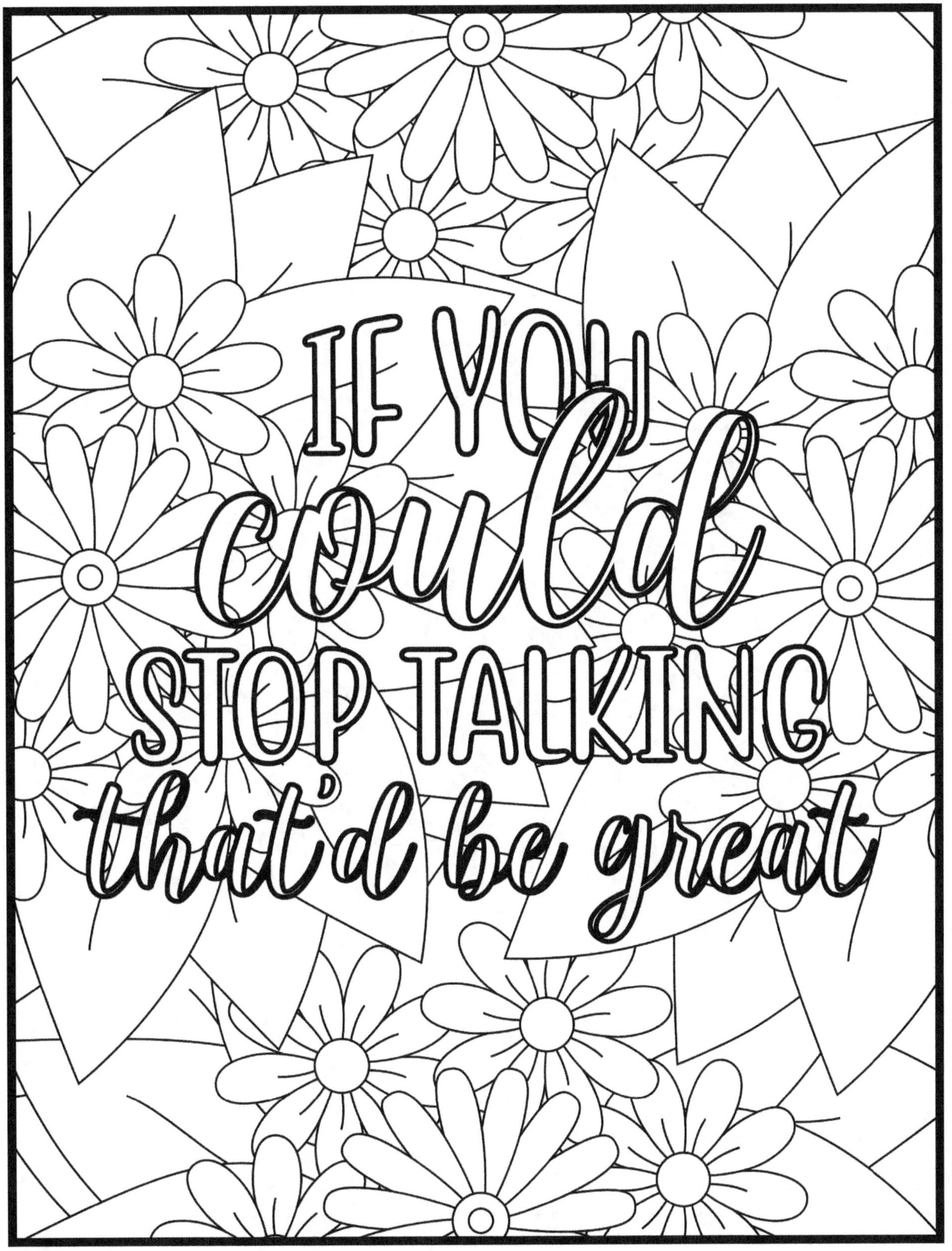
IF YOU
could
STOP TALKING
that'd be great

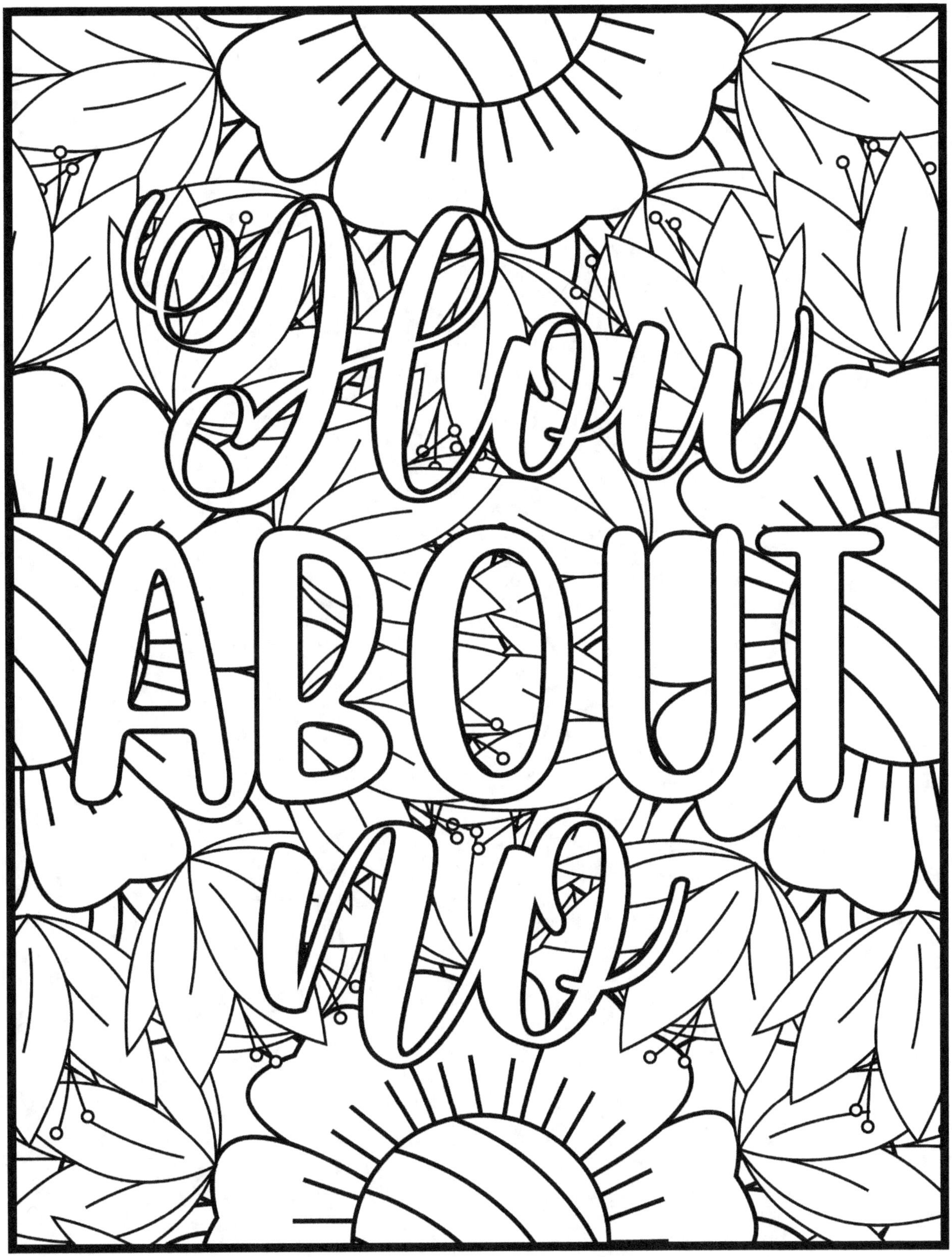
How
ABOUT
no

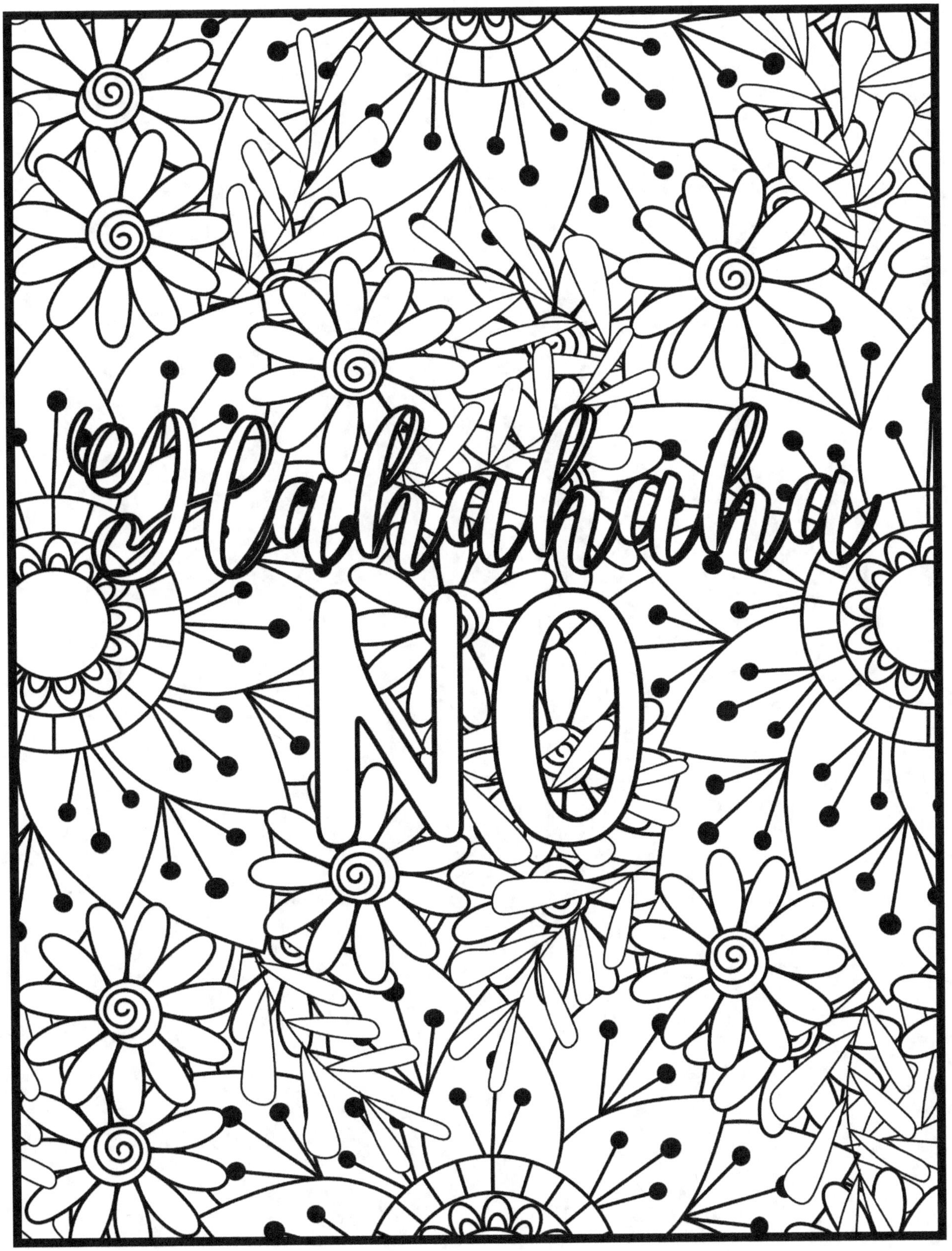
Hahahaha
NO

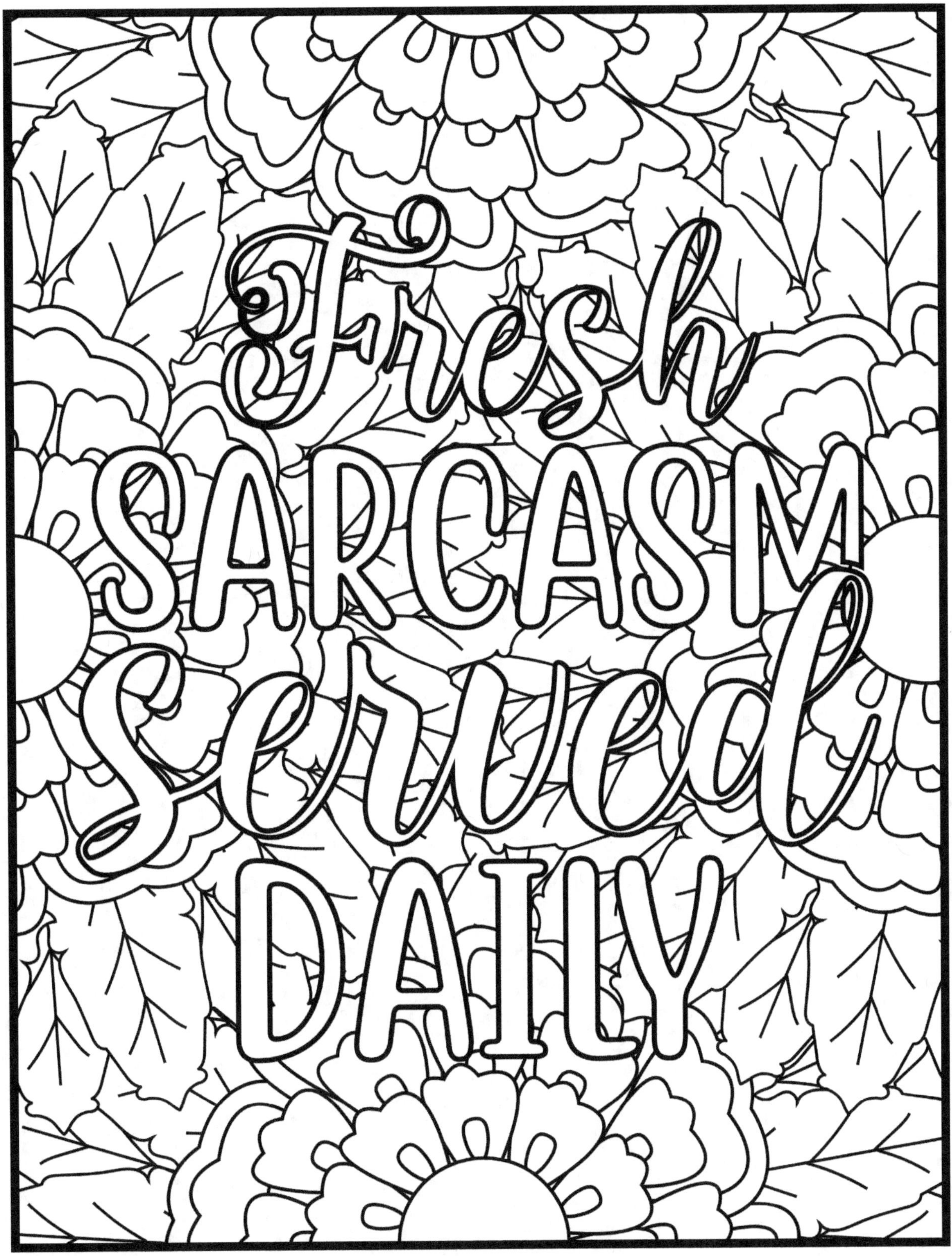
Fresh
SARCASM
Served
DAILY

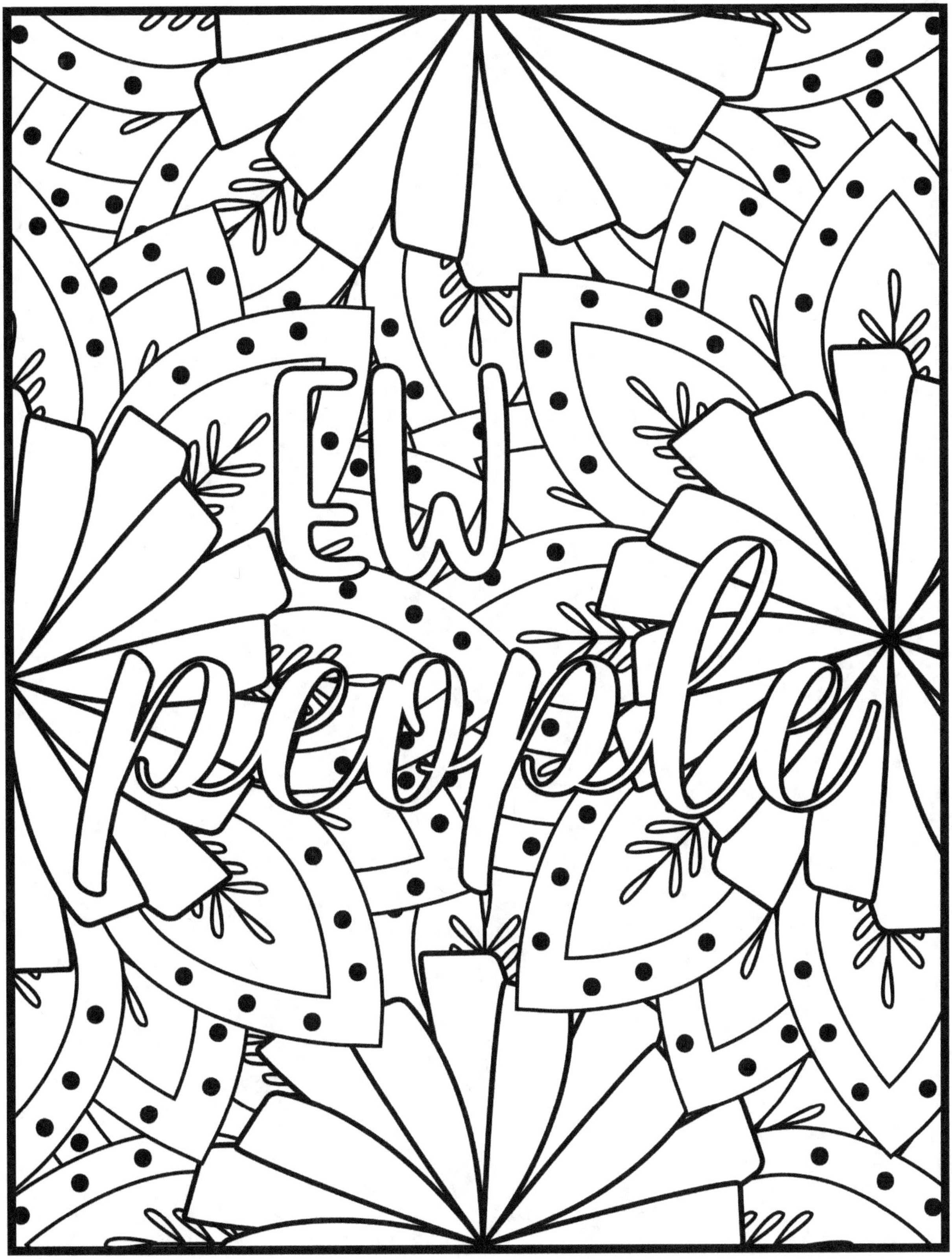
Ew
people

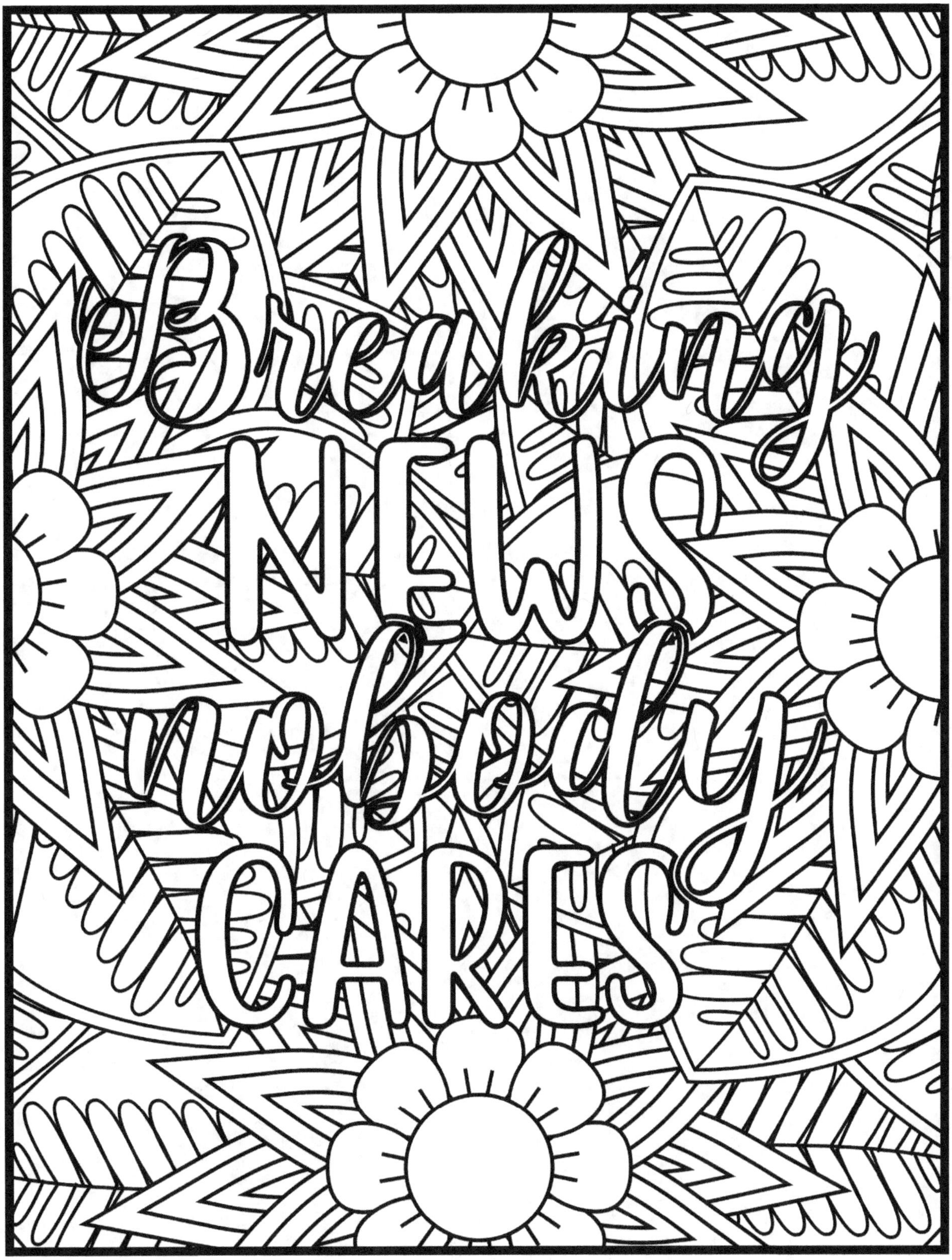
Breaking
NEWS
nobody
CARES

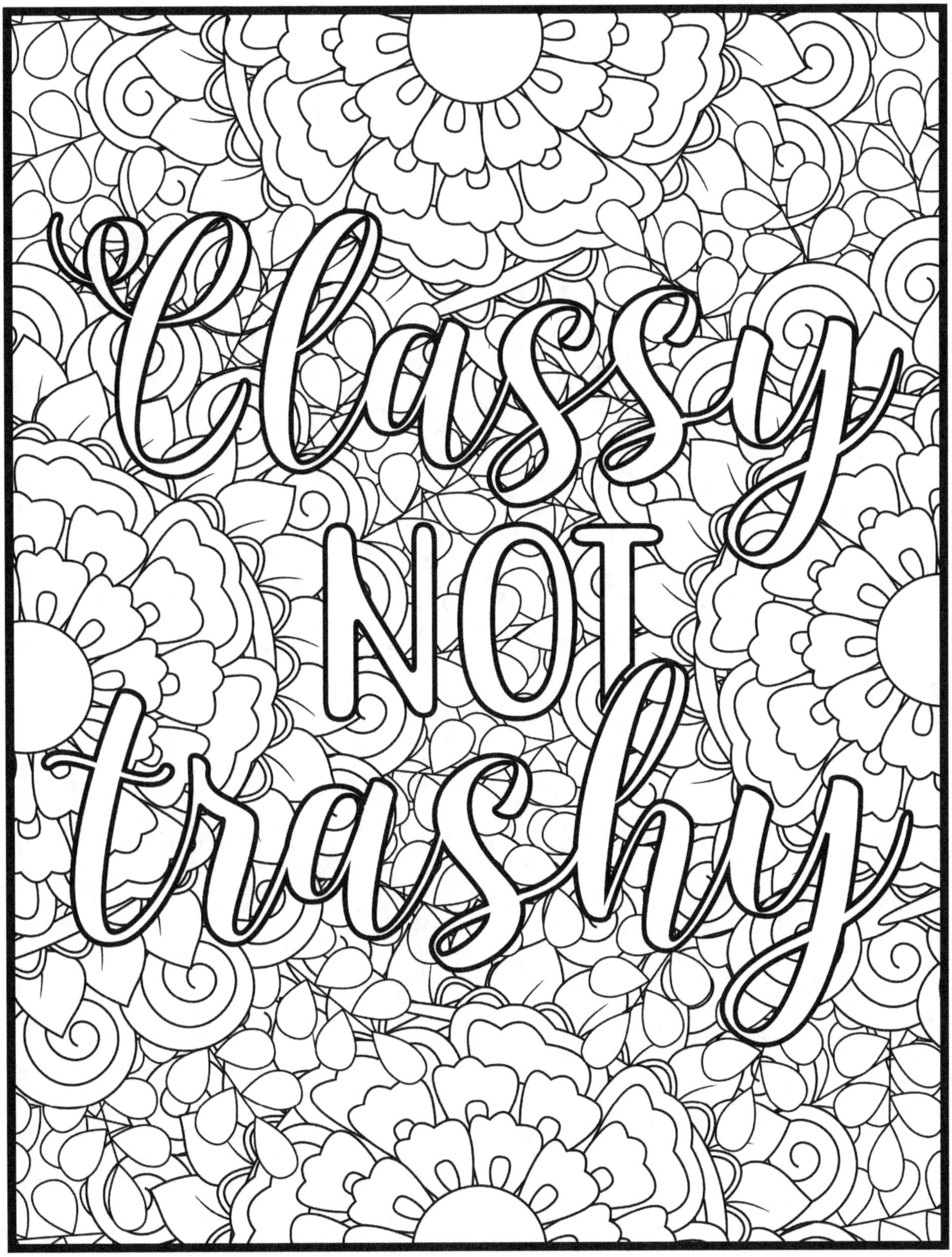
Classy
NOT
trashy

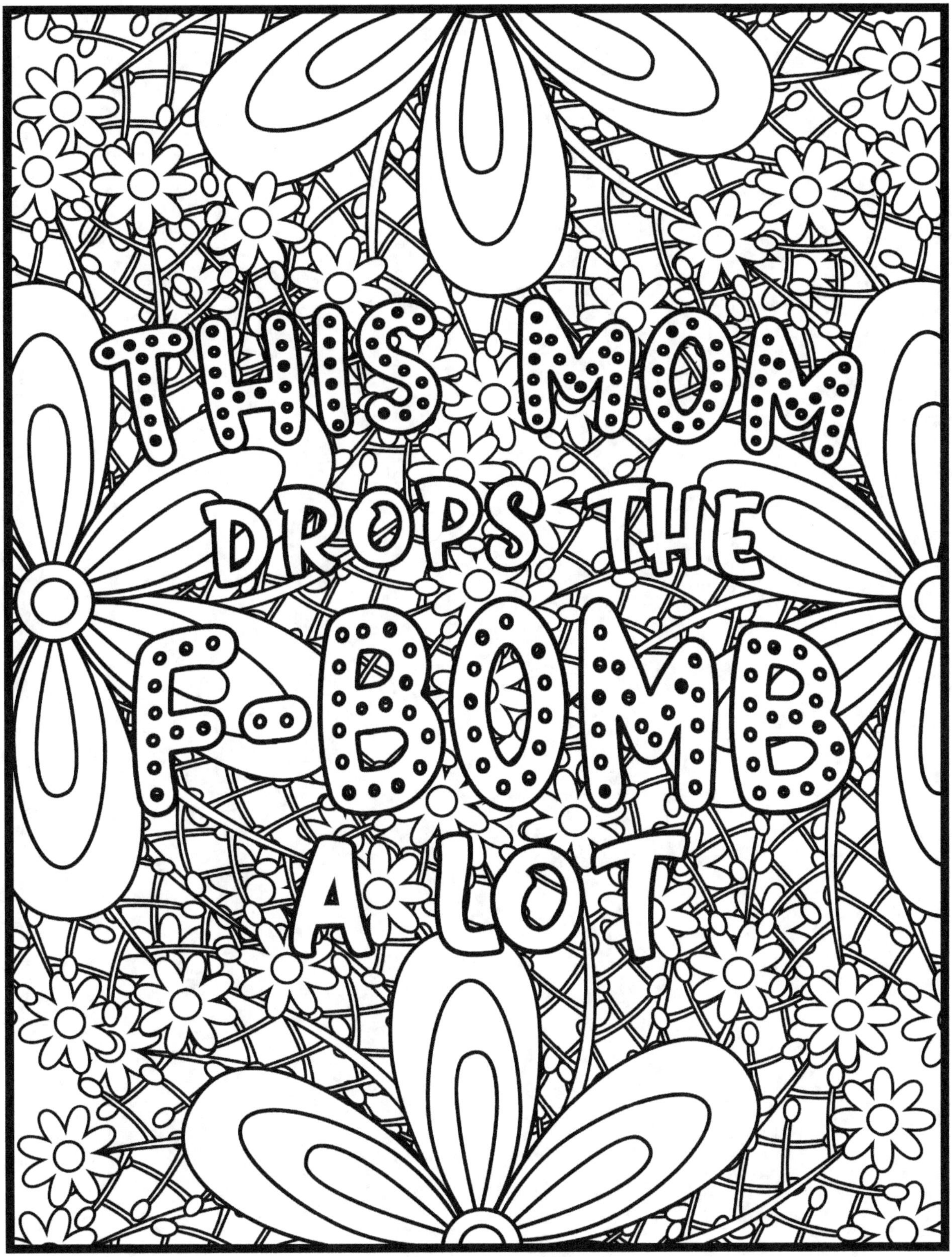
THIS MOM
DROPS THE
F-BOMB
A LOT

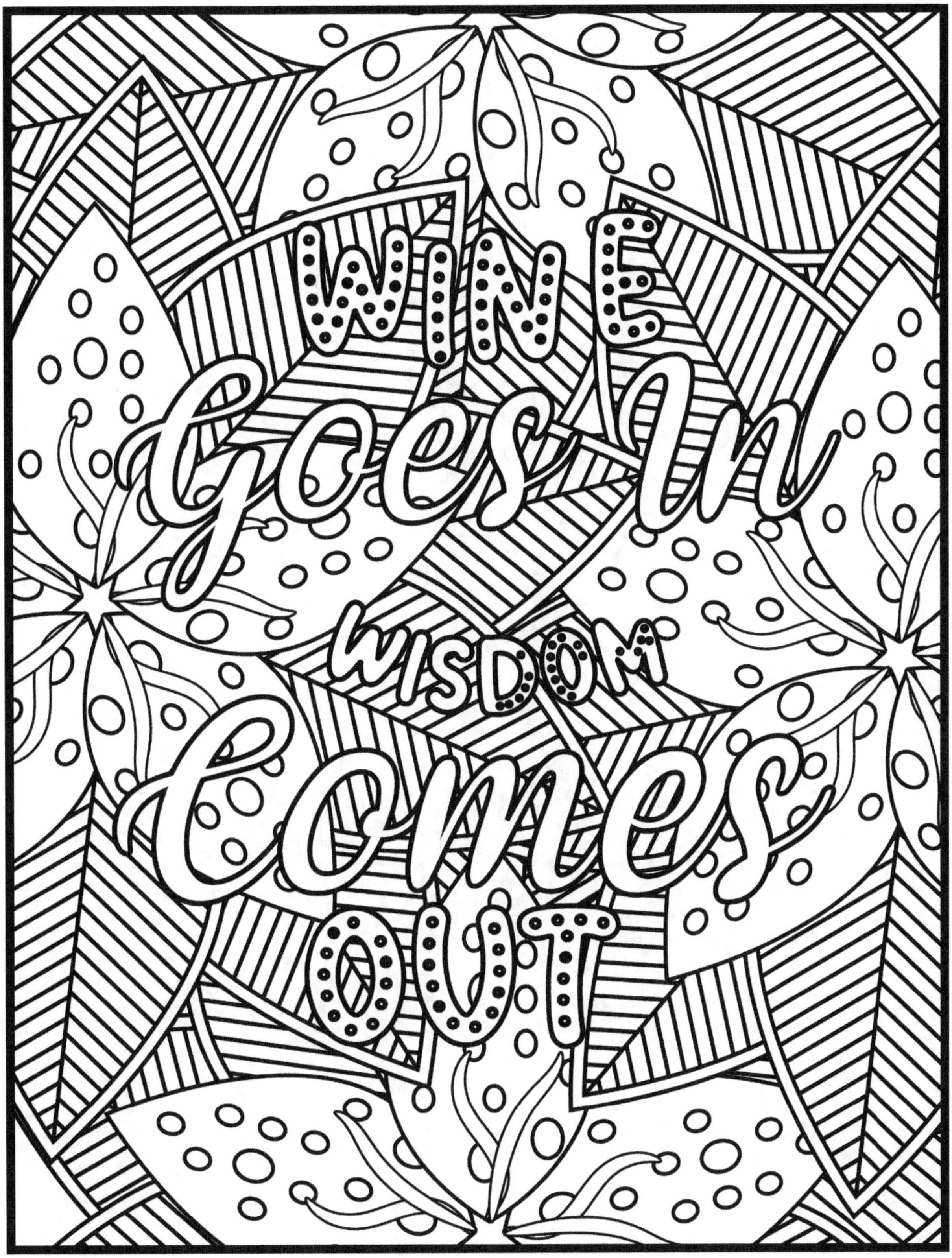
WINE
Goes In
WISDOM
Comes
OUT

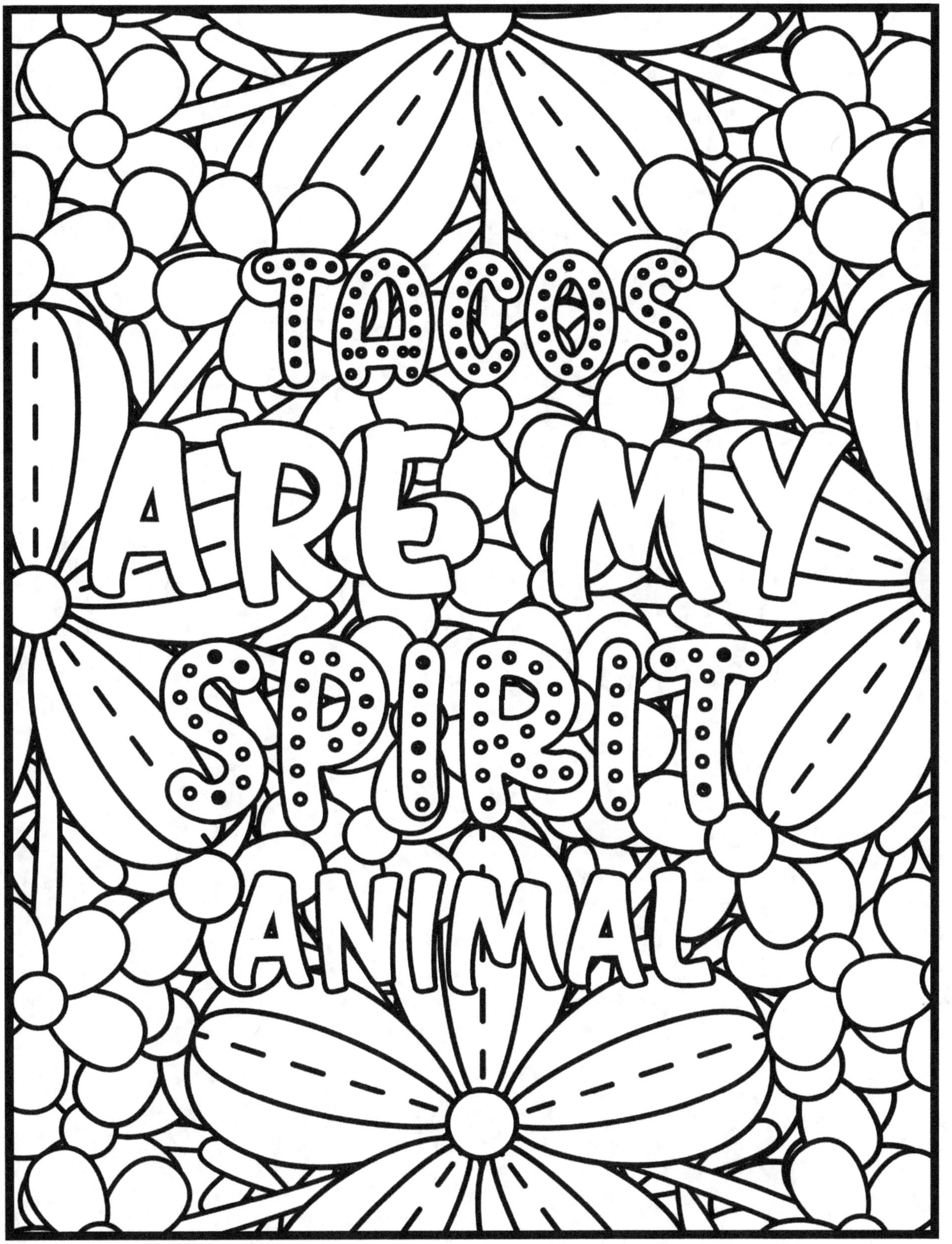
TACOS
ARE MY
SPIRIT
ANIMAL

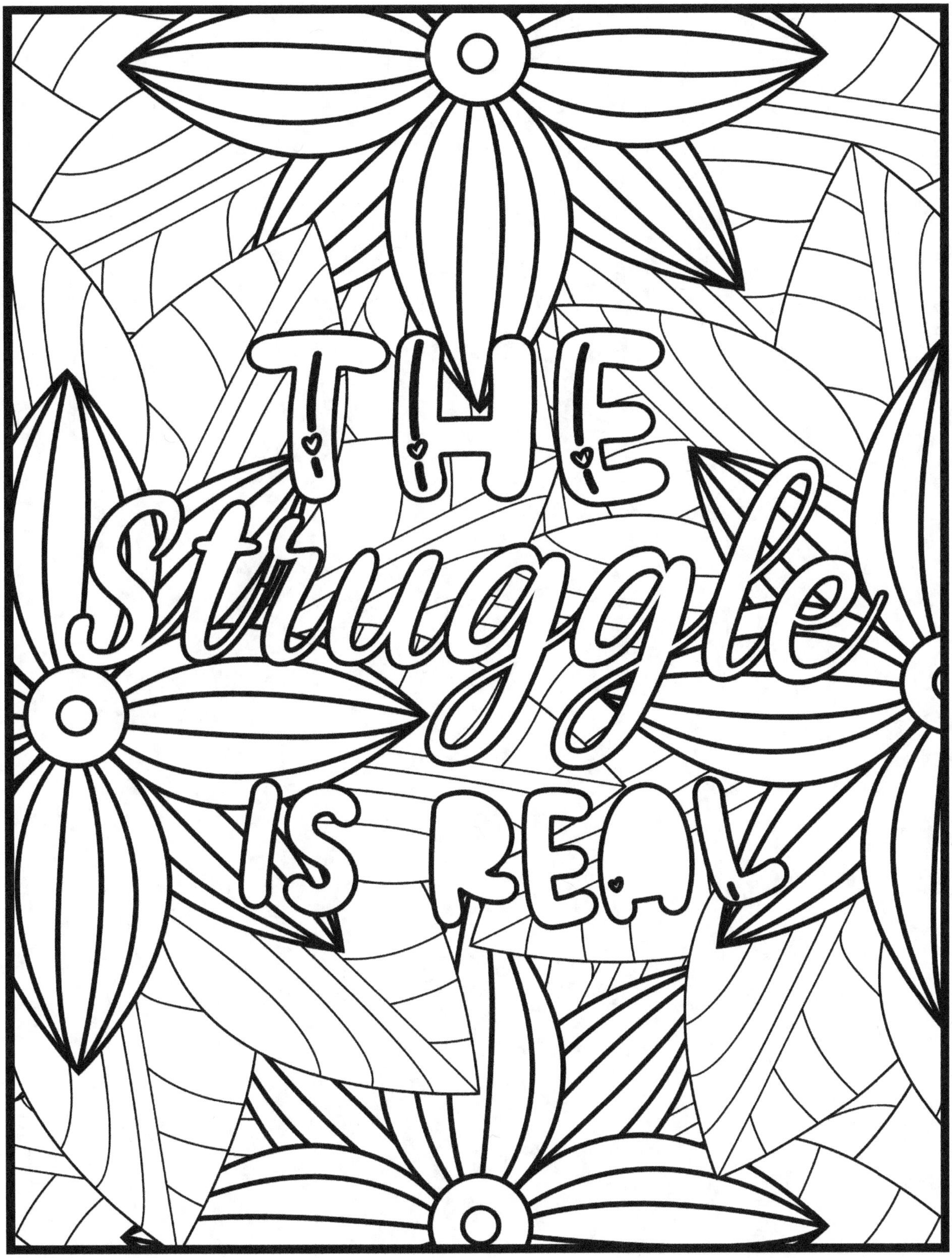
THE
Struggle
IS REAL

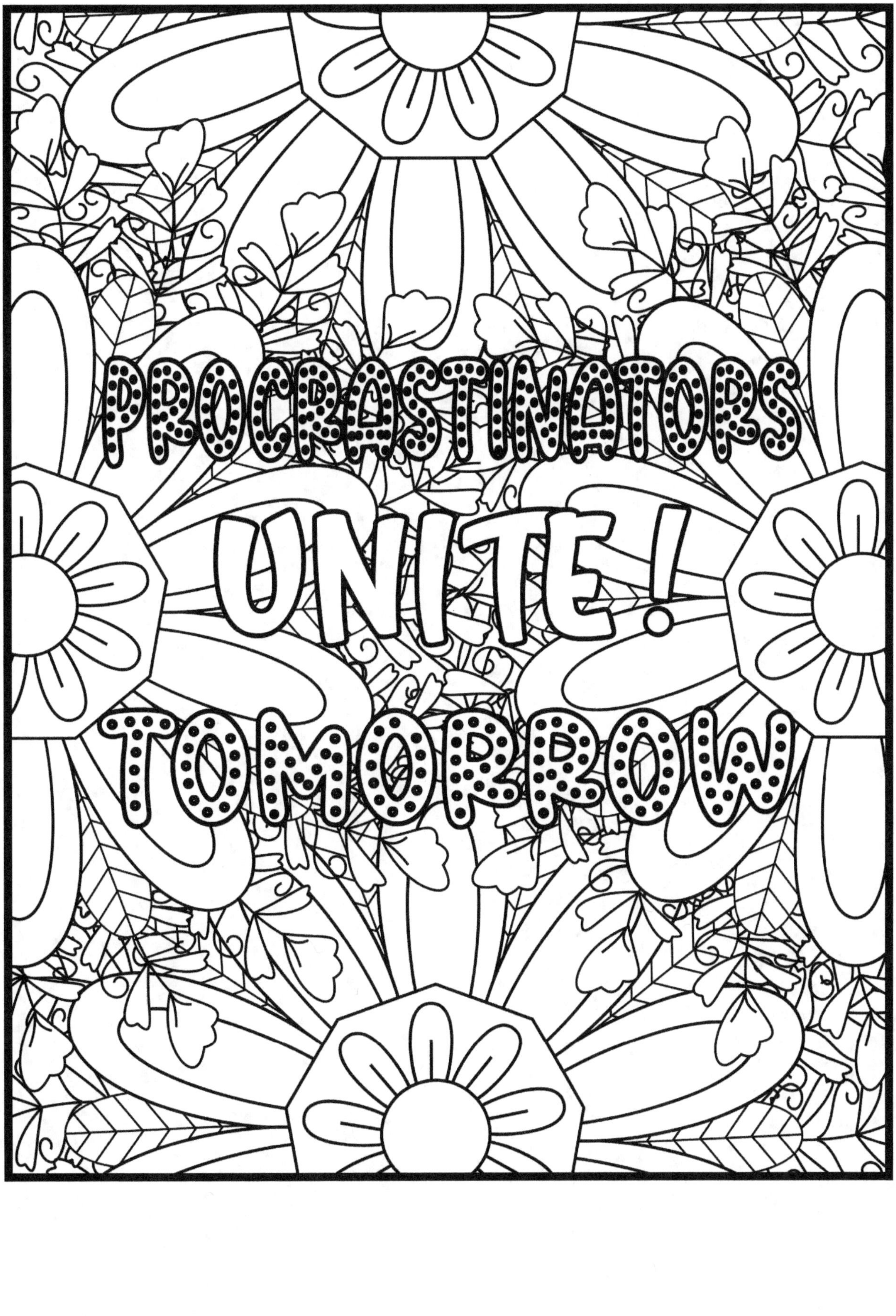
PROCRASTINATORS
UNITE!
TOMORROW

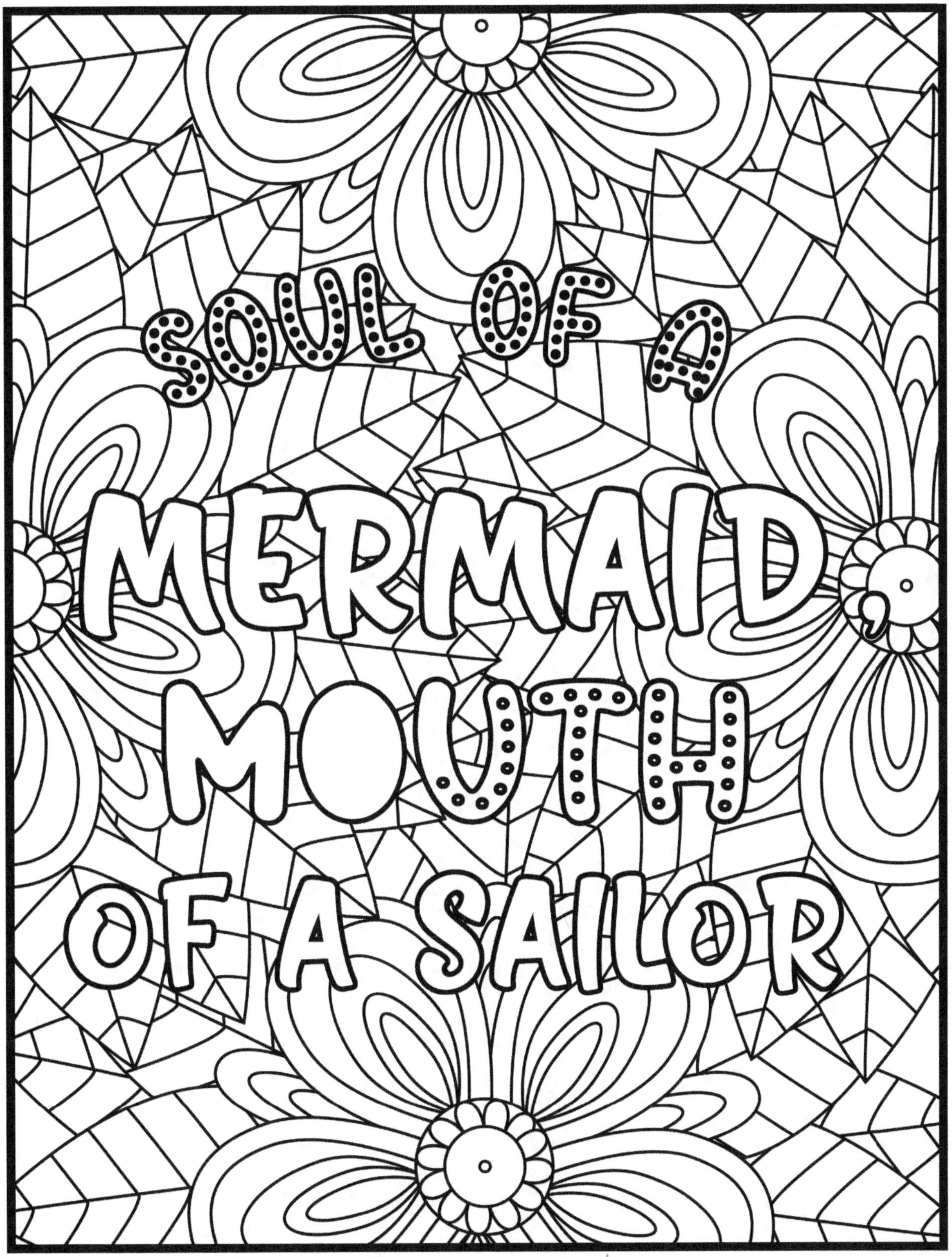
SOUL OF A
MERMAID,
MOUTH
OF A SAILOR

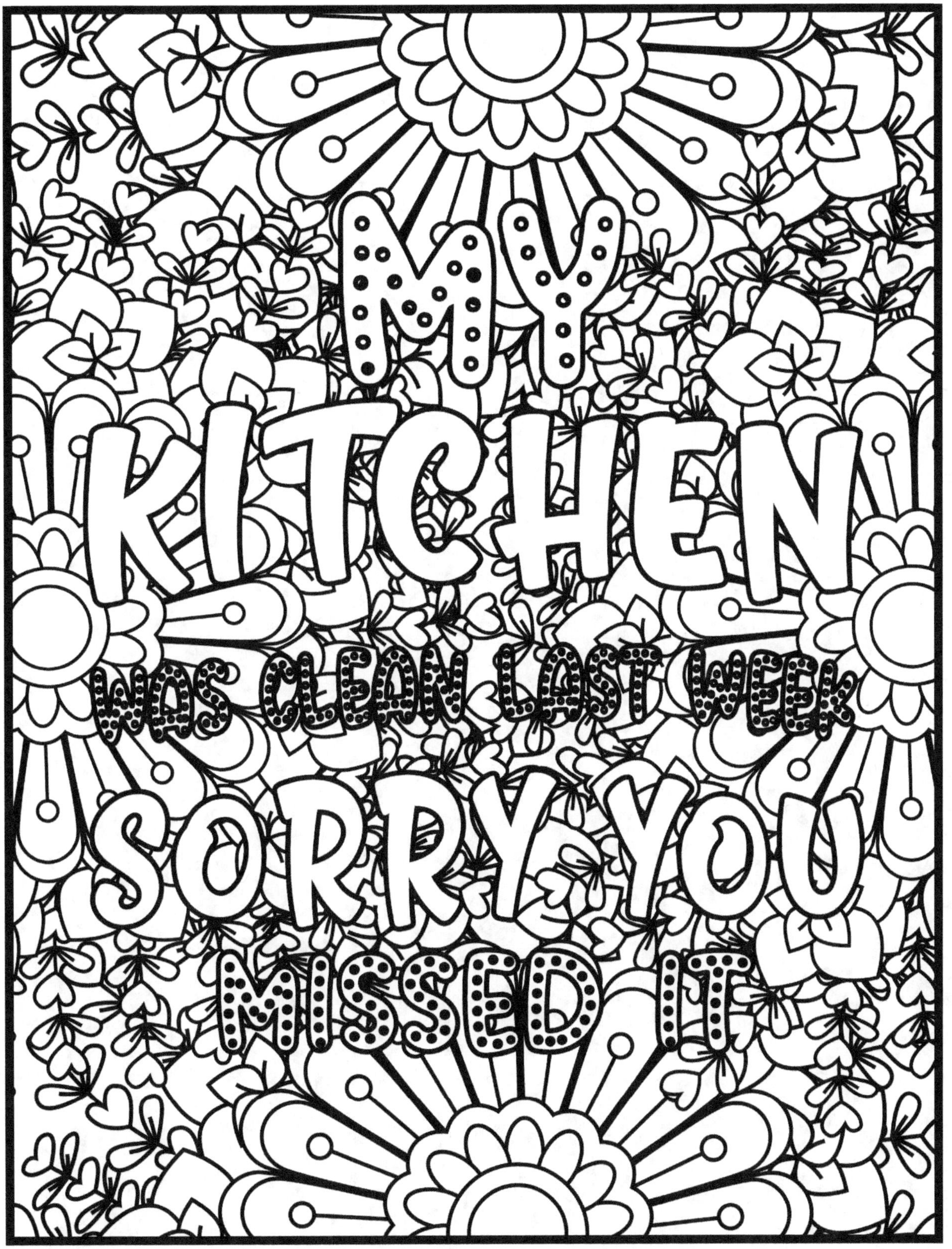
MY
KITCHEN
WAS CLEAN LAST WEEK
SORRY YOU
MISSED IT

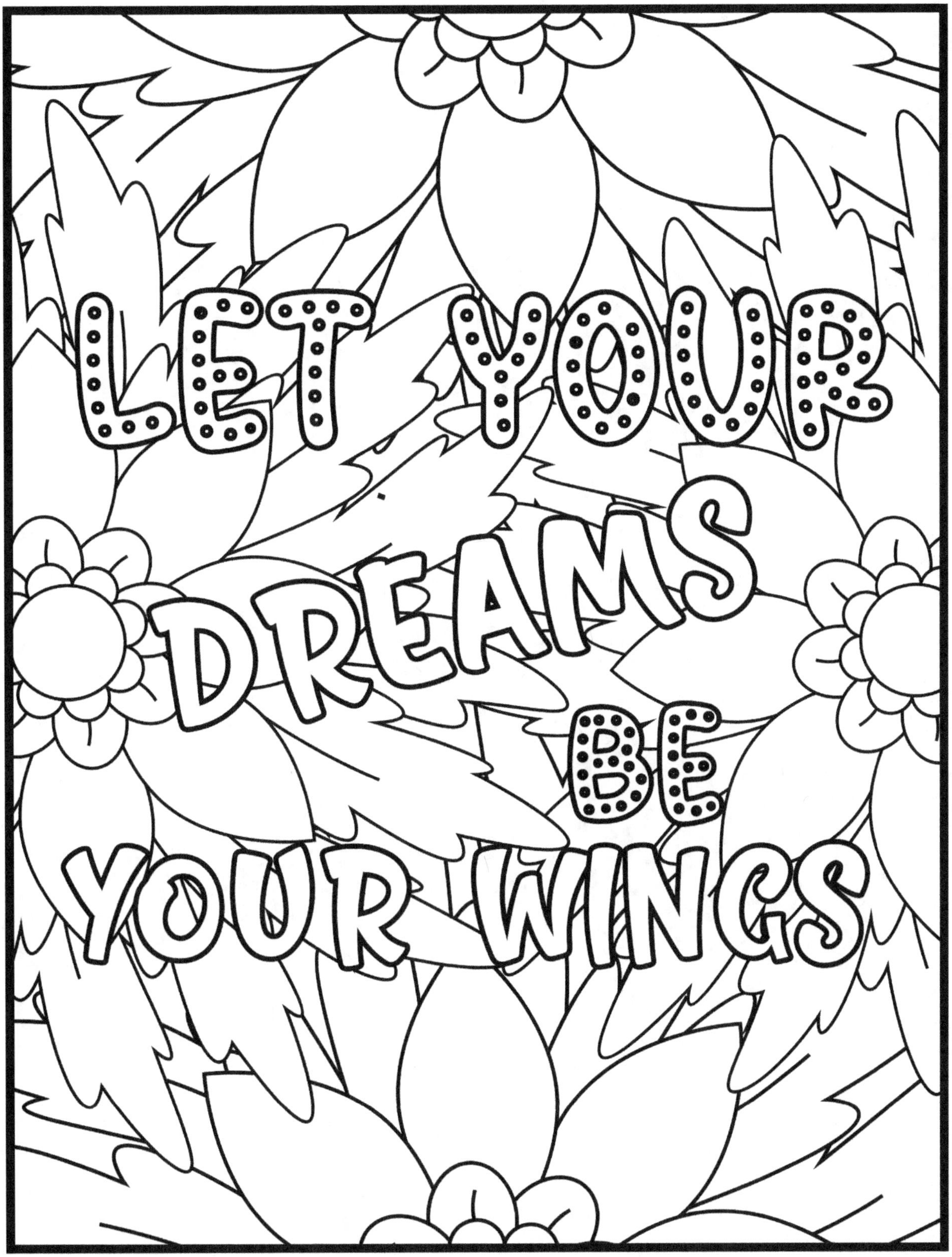
LET YOUR
DREAMS
BE
YOUR WINGS

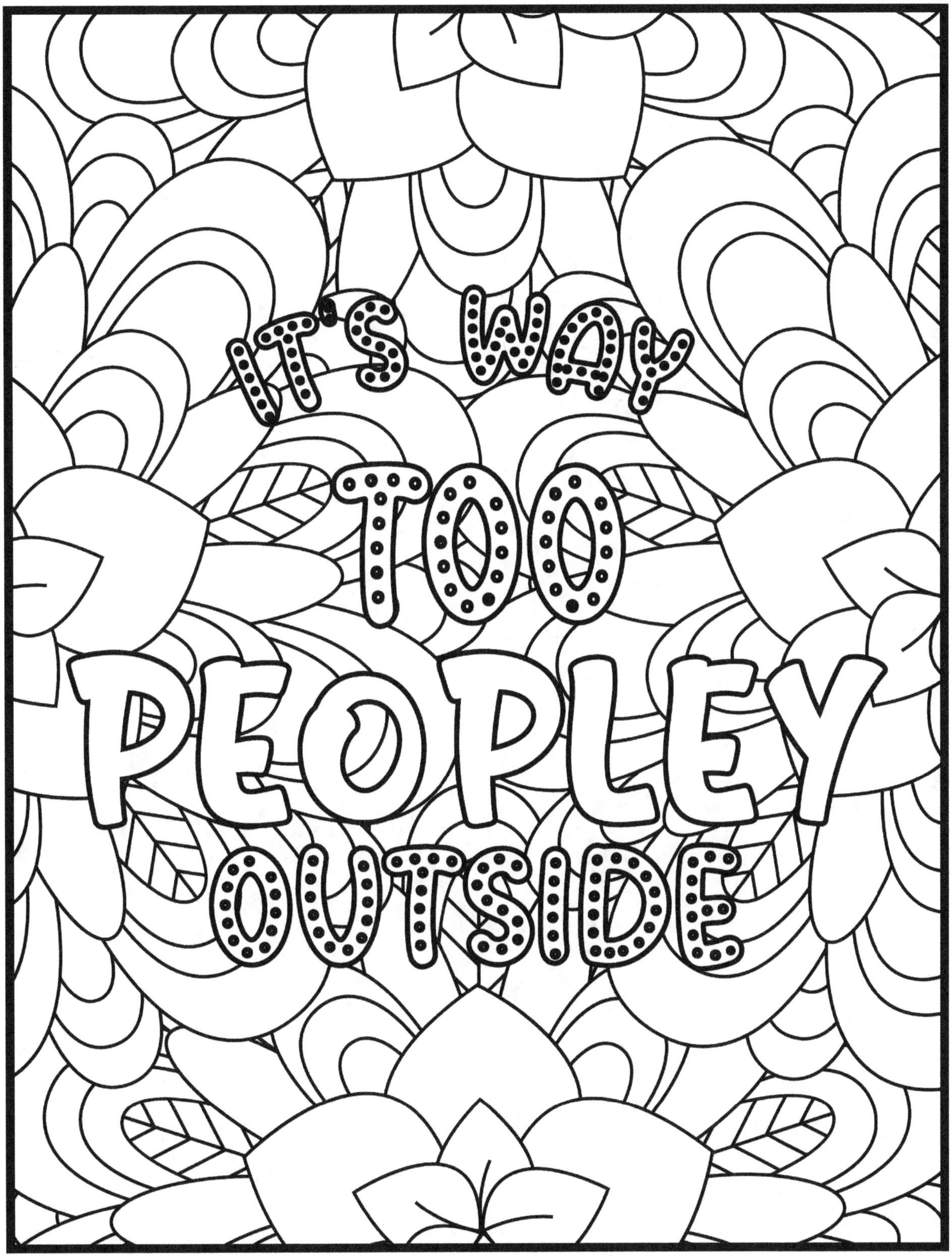
IT'S WAY
TOO
PEOPLEY
OUTSIDE

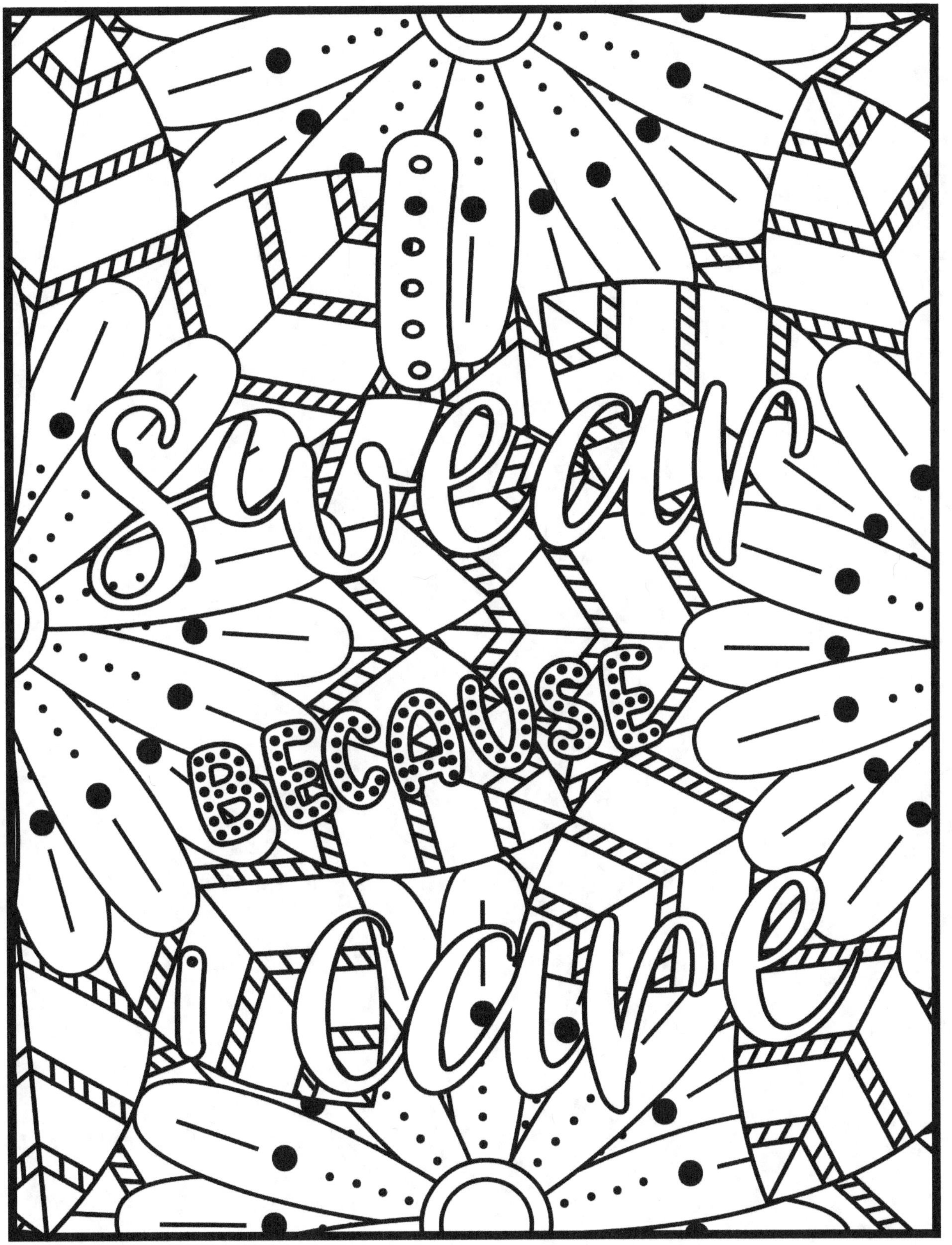
Swear
BECAUSE
i care

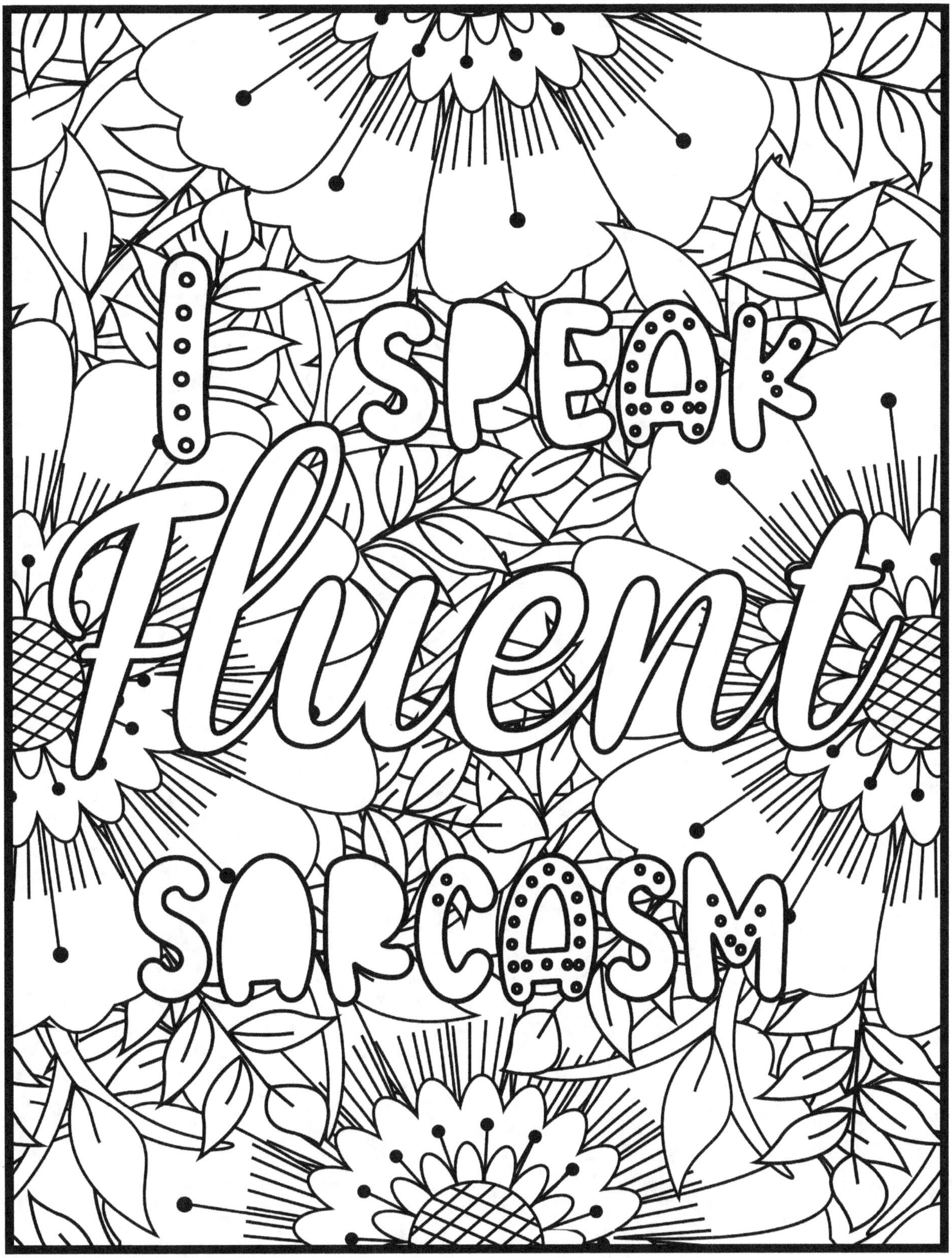
I SPEAK
Fluent
SARCASM

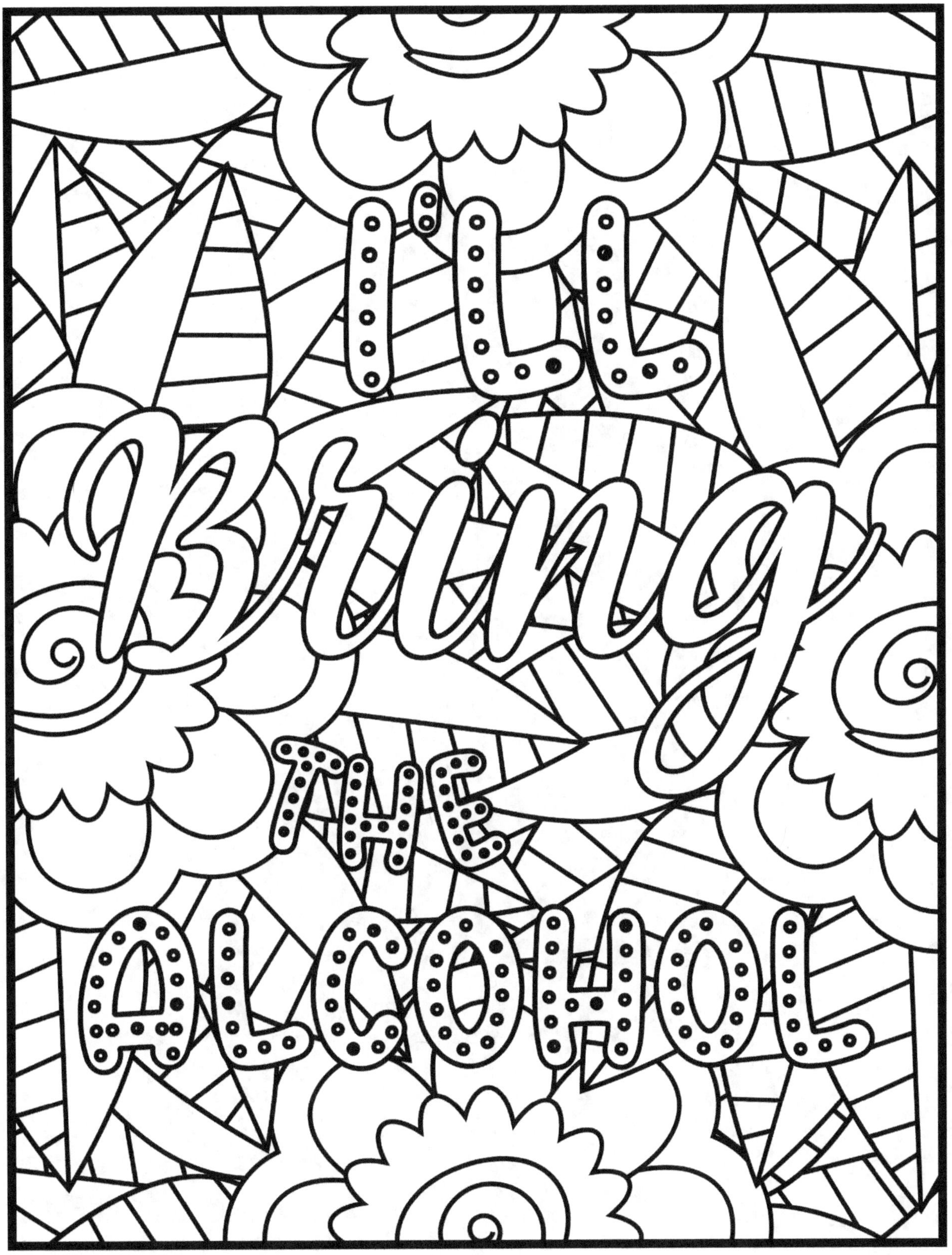
I'LL
Bring
THE
ALCOHOL

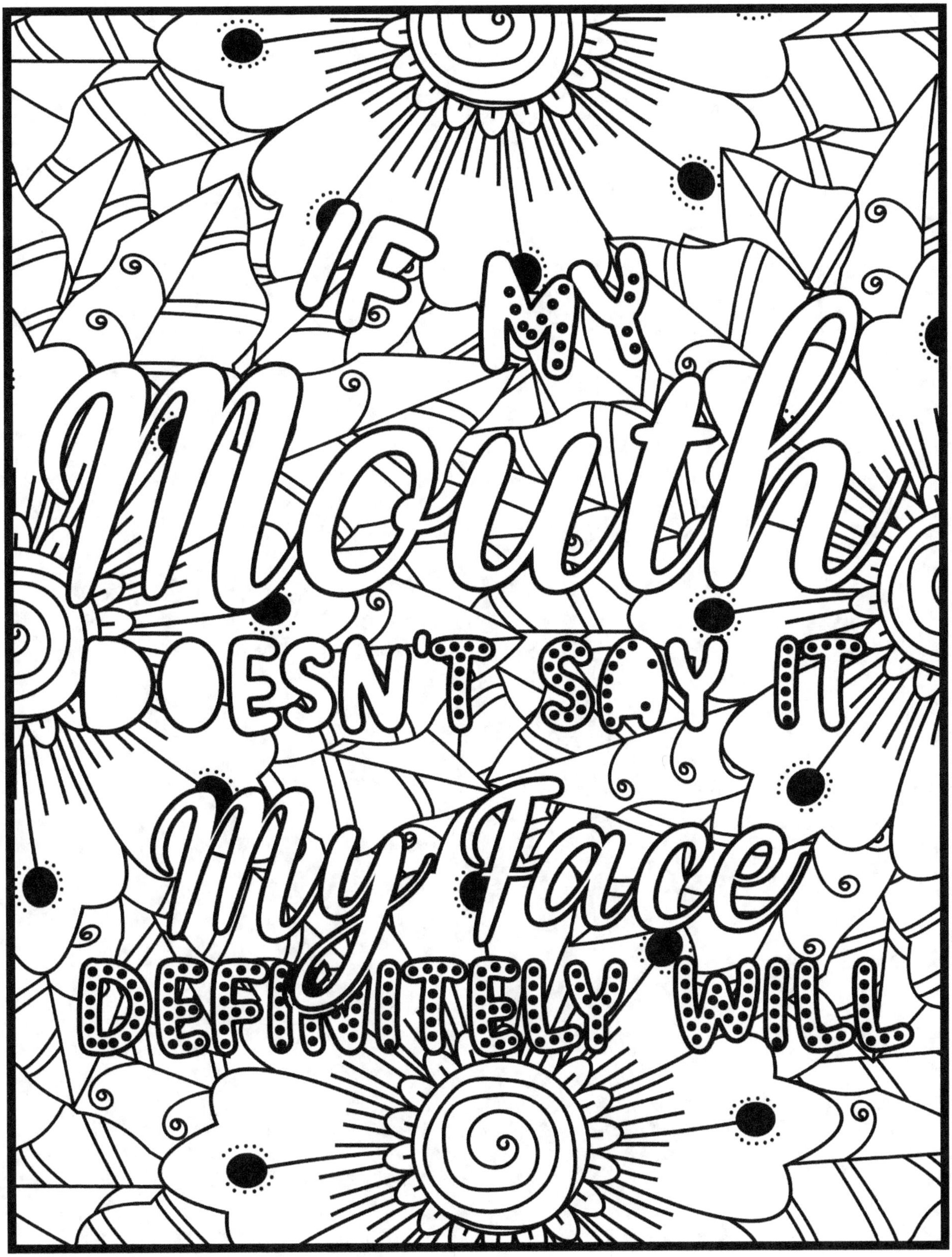
IF MY
Mouth
DOESN'T SAY IT
My Face
DEFINITELY WILL

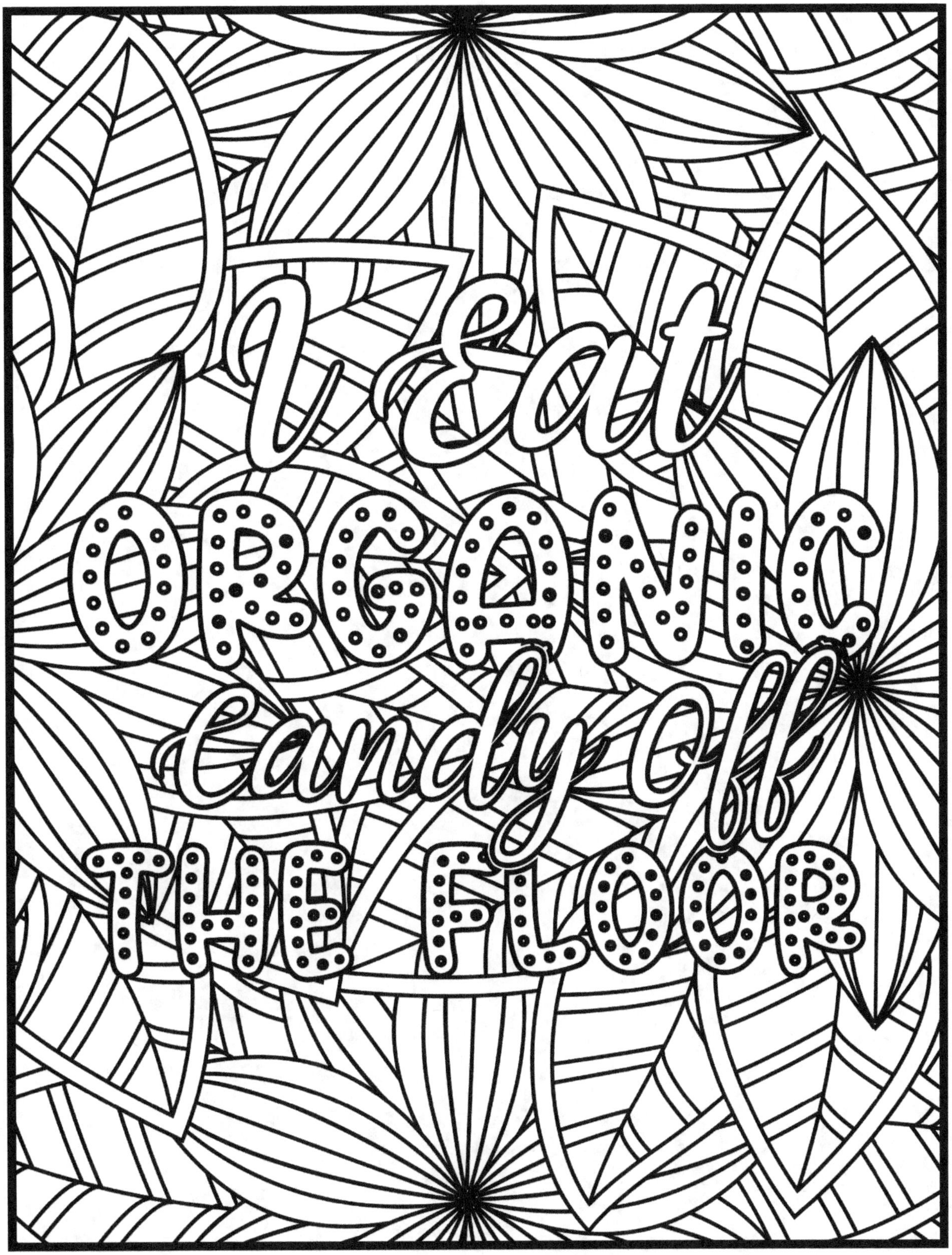
I Eat
ORGANIC
Candy Off
THE FLOOR

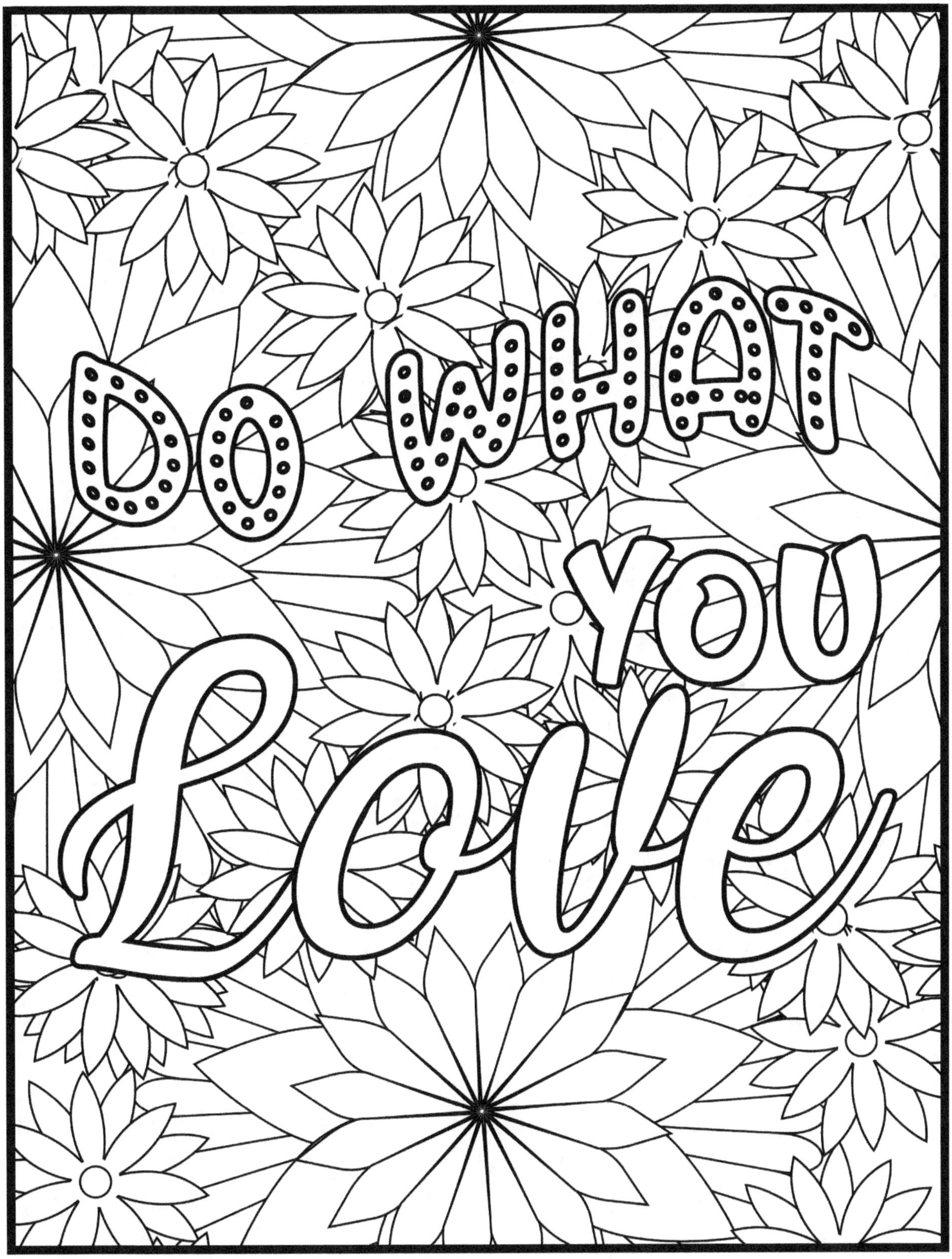
DO WHAT
YOU
Love

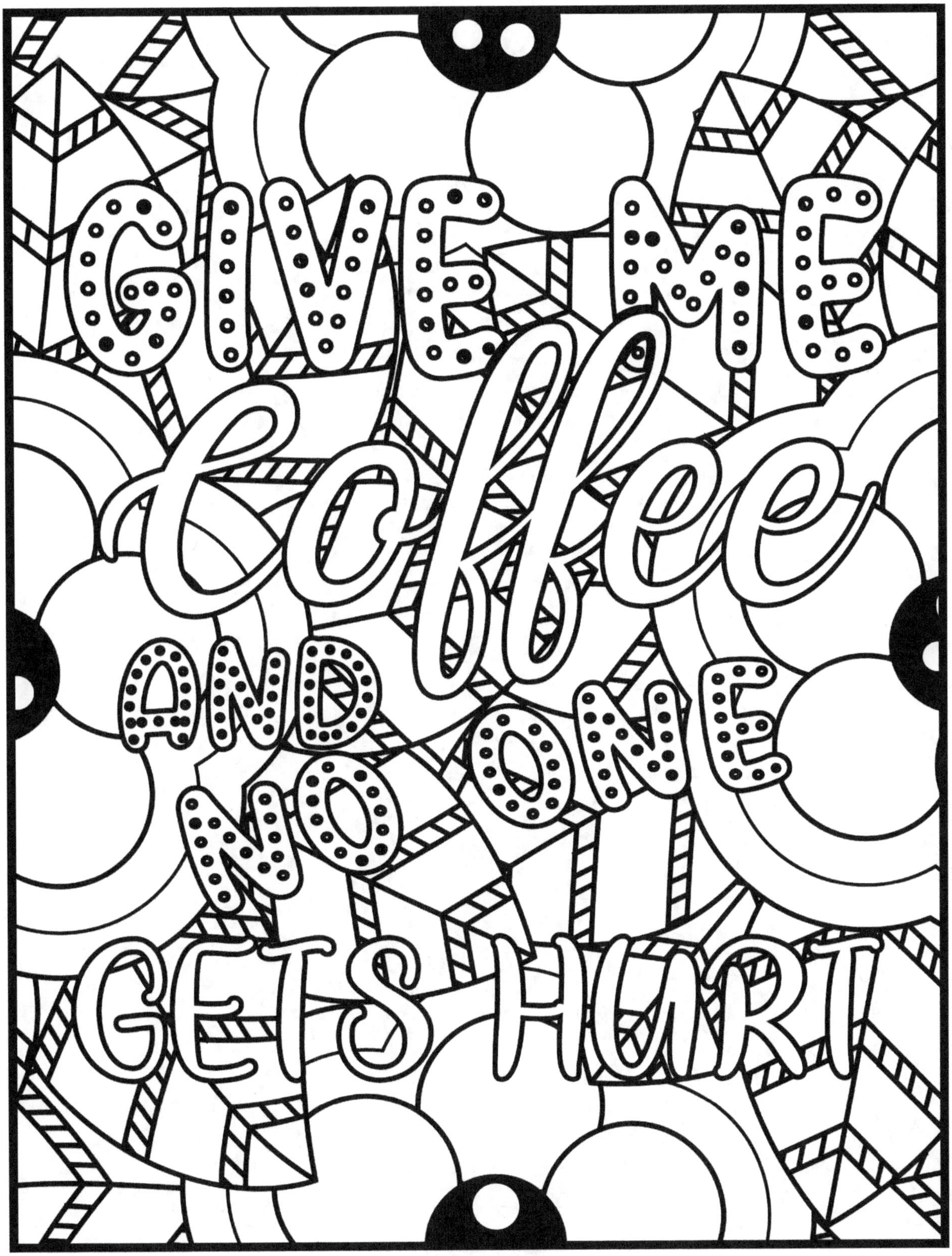
GIVE ME
Coffee
AND NO ONE
GETS HURT

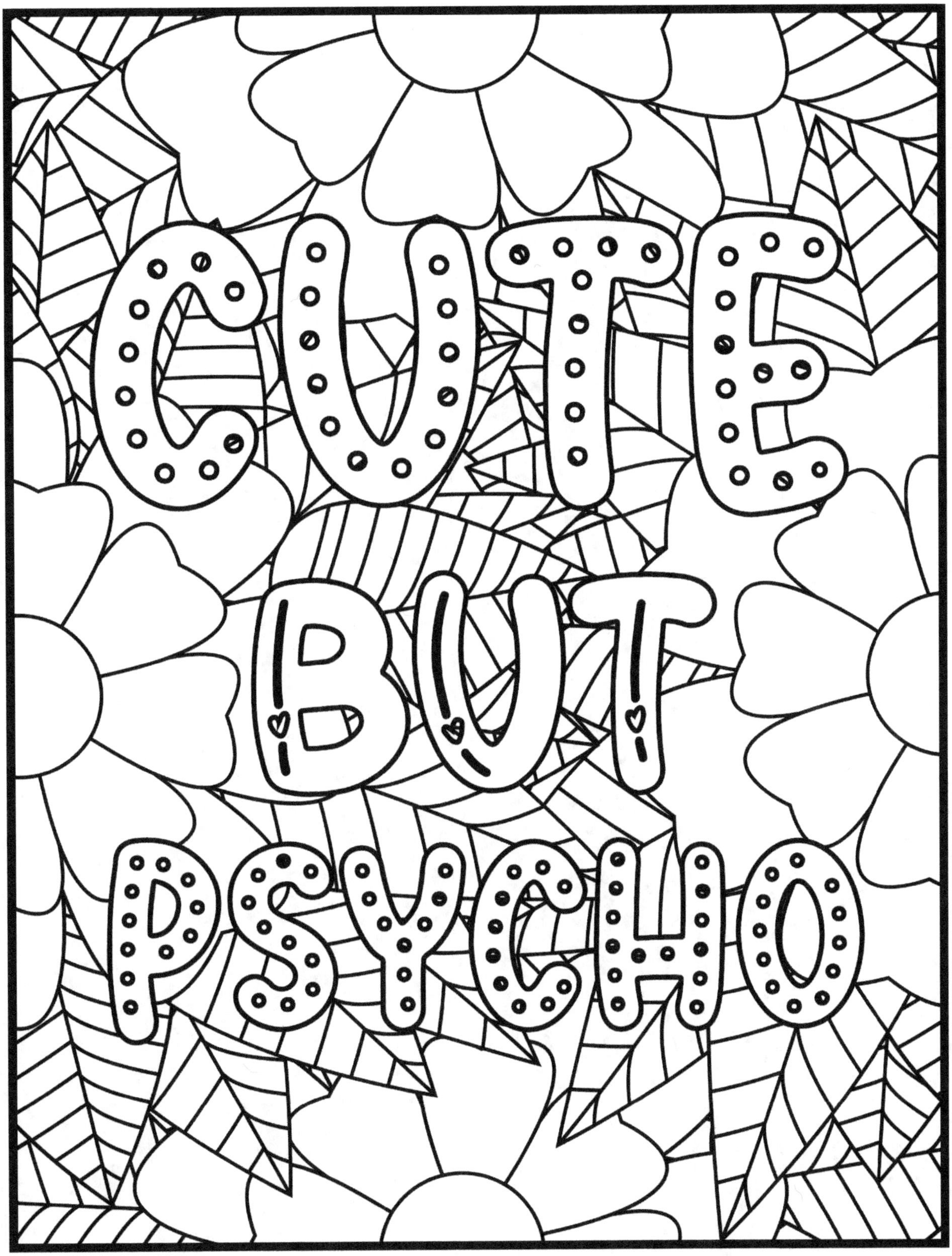
CUTE
BUT
PSYCHO

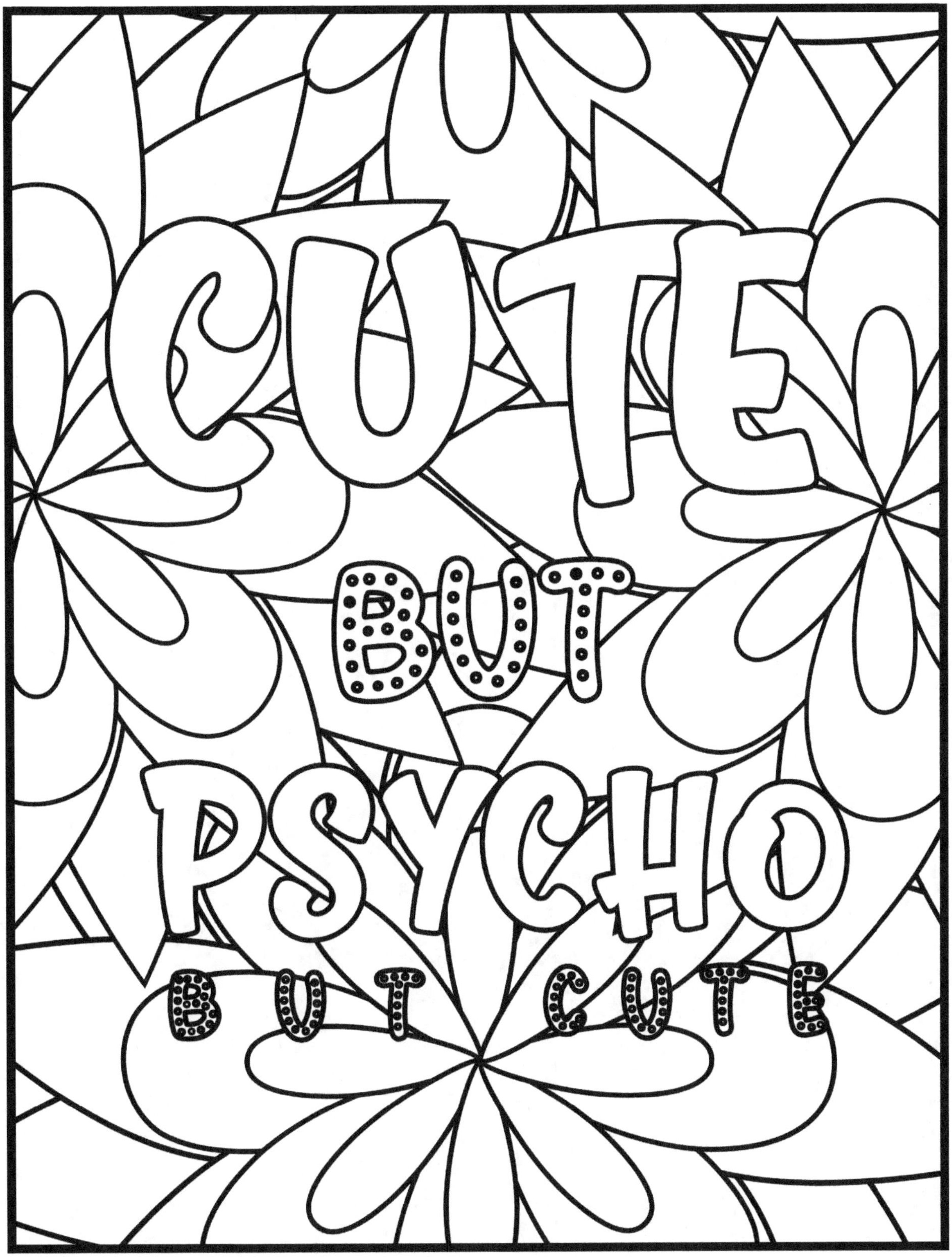
CUTE
BUT
PSYCHO
BUT CUTE

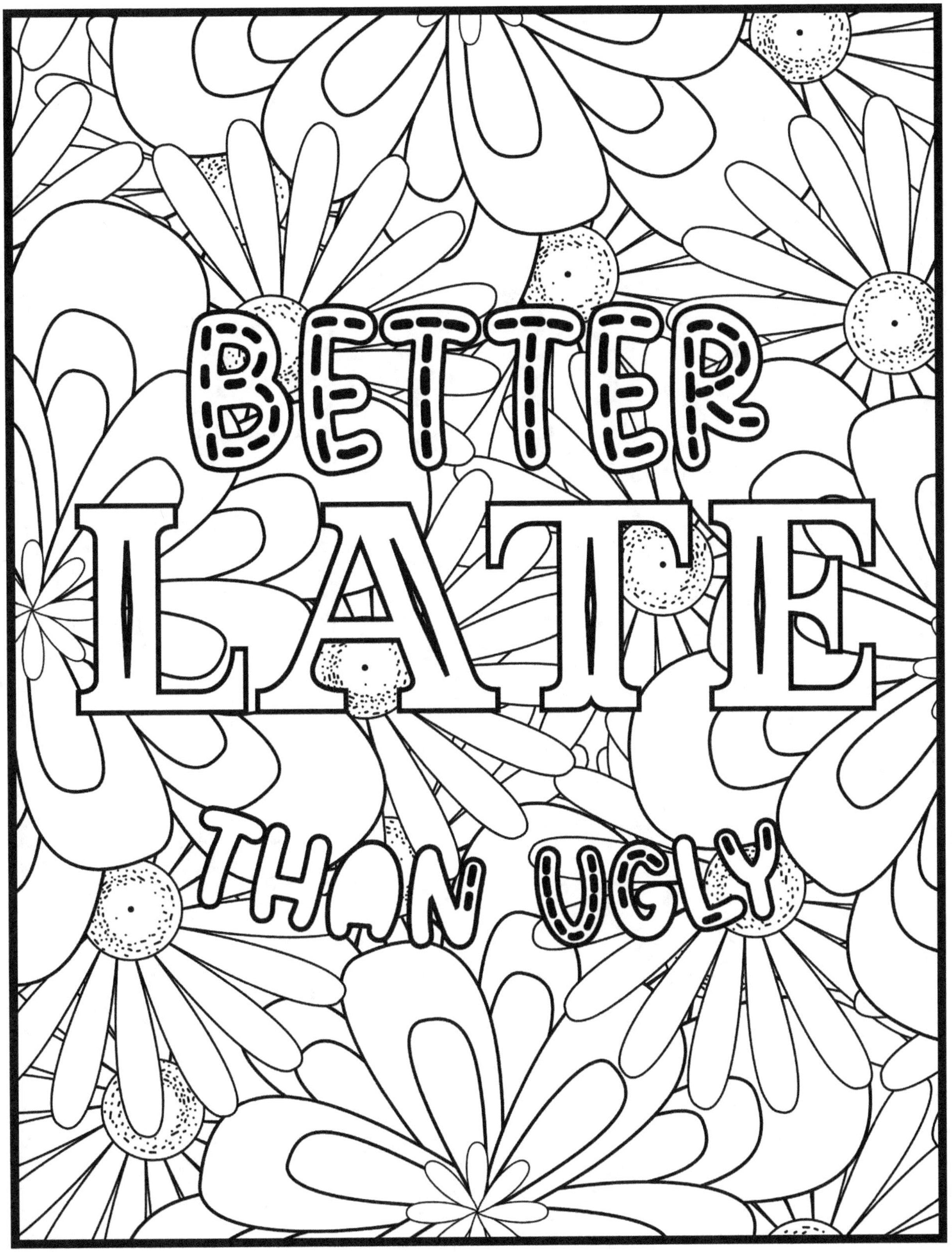
BETTER
LATE
THAN UGLY

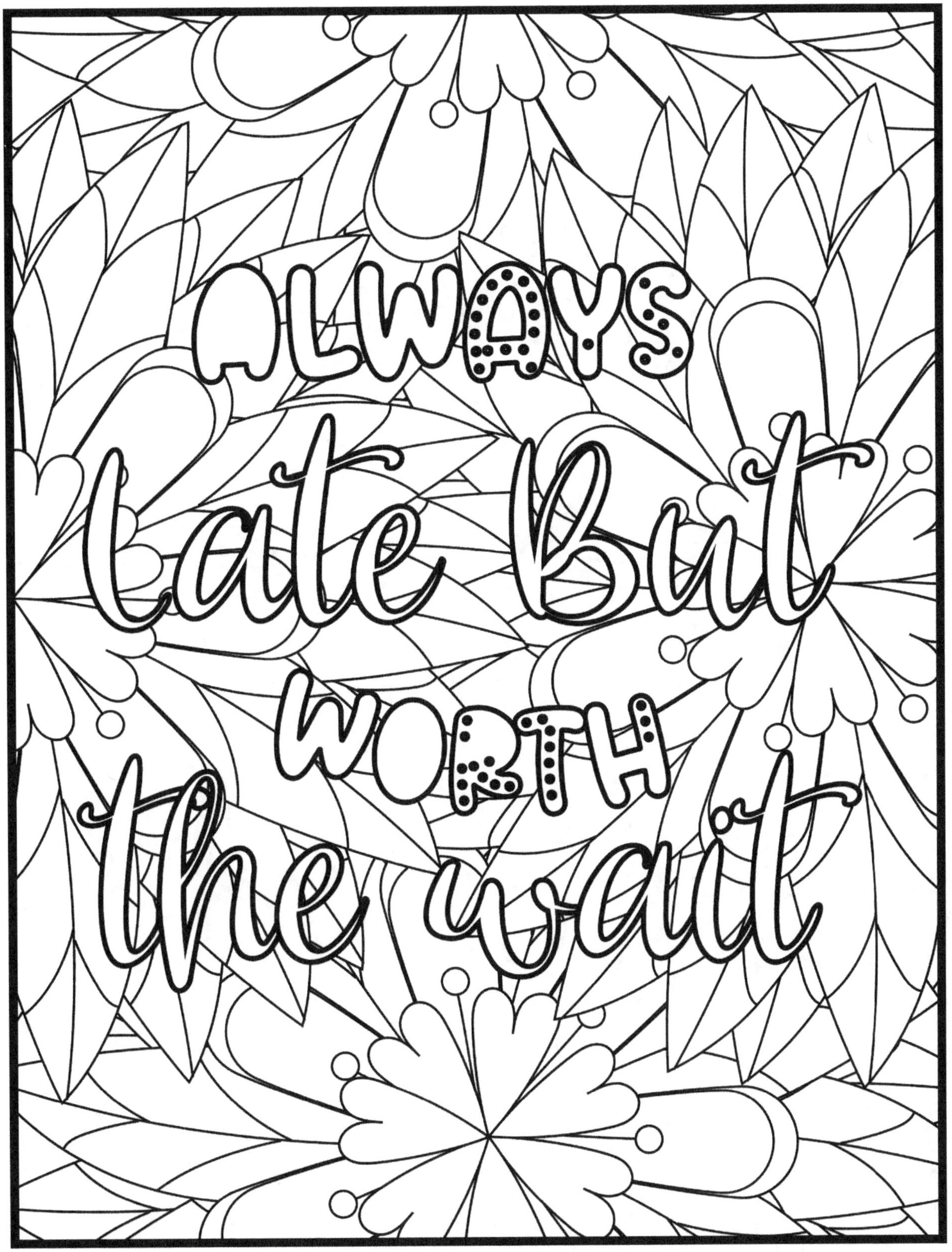
ALWAYS
Late But
WORTH
the wait

www.ingramcontent.com/pod-product-compliance
Lightning Source LLC
Chambersburg PA
CBHW060000230526
45472CB00008B/1888